Learning

to

Listen

Learning

to

Listen

JoAnn Yops

Community, Inc.
Troy, Michigan

Community, Inc.
P.O. Box 1193
Troy, Michigan 48099-1193

Publisher's Cataloging in Publication
 (Prepared by Quality Books Inc.)

Yops, JoAnn.
        Learning to Listen / JoAnn Yops.
        p. cm.
        ISBN: 1-886534-00-4

1. Listening. 2. Counseling. 3. Crisis Intervention
(Psychiatry) 4. Suicide-Prevention.   I. Title.

BF323.L5Y67 1995   153.6'8
                                                        QBI95-20305

Dedication

This book was inspired by and is dedicated to the love of my life, my dear husband Rich, in whom I both see and feel the love of God personified.

Acknowledgments

This book would never have happened without the loving support and encouragement of my husband Rich, who tirelessly composed and recomposed it on the computer. My heartfelt appreciation also extends to Sylvia Smith Frantz, my mother and friend, for proofreading and offering valuable feedback with the wit and humor for which she is well-known. Finally, I am grateful for the illustrations of Michael Robinson, who so perfectly captures the emotions of his delightful characters.

CONTENTS

CONTENTS (cont'd)

INTRODUCTION

The fact that you are reading this book indicates that you are the type of person most of us would love to have as a friend. You are by nature a compassionate person who is genuinely interested in helping others through difficult times. William J. Bennett, in *The Book of Virtues,* defines compassion as "a virtue that takes seriously the reality of other persons, their inner lives, their emotions, as well as their external circumstances. It is an active disposition toward fellowship and sharing, toward supportive companionship in distress or in woe."

The ultimate expression of compassion comes in the form of a focused ear and an empathic heart. Listening is an acquired skill which many people never learn. It consists primarily of empathy, which means vicariously experiencing the feelings of another person.

There are times in everyone's life when we wish someone understood what we were feeling and could provide an ear to listen. Too often the search for a listener is fruitless, and we are left feeling isolated and alone to cope as best we can. However, if we find an empathic listener, our burden is lightened. We find in the process the seed which allows our encounters to draw us closer, that nourish meaningful exchange and encourage our relationships to blossom. That seed is empathy. Empathy establishes trust. Empathy communicates understanding and concern. Empathy touches the heart.

This book provides both the concepts and the vocabulary. It includes sections on crisis intervention and suicide, followed by a vocabulary section consisting of over 850 'feeling' words, empathic phrases, and illustrations. The value of empathy and the way to communicate it are clearly defined.

You may be reading this as a supplemental text for a counseling course or crisis intervention training class. Perhaps you simply wish to enhance communication with loved ones. Whatever the reason, you will see dramatic improvements in all your personal relationships as a result of integrating these skills into your daily life. May you be blessed in your endeavors.

LISTEN

(Anonymous)

When I ask you to listen to me and you
start giving advice,
you have not done what I asked.
When I ask you to listen to me and you
begin to tell me why
I shouldn't feel that way, you are
trampling on my feelings.
When I ask you to listen to me and you
feel you have to do
something to solve my problems, you
have failed me,
strange as that may seem.
Perhaps that's why prayer works for
some people.
Because
God is mute and He doesn't offer advice
or try to fix things.
He just listens and trusts you to work
it out for yourself.
So please, just listen and hear me. And
if you want to talk,
wait a few minutes for your turn and I
promise I'll listen to you.

1. LEARNING TO LISTEN

Active Listening

Active listening is a learned skill few of us were ever taught. Have you ever sat among a group of people and observed the conversation process? A lot of people may be talking, but is anyone truly listening? What I see most often is the "listener" waiting for the "speaker" to finish (or at least pause) so the "listener" can relate a personal experience that often has little to do with what the "speaker" just said. Did the speaker perhaps bare her* soul, only to be ignored or outdone by the listener's tale? Could this demoralizing occurrence be the reason so many people tend to withdraw in social settings or family affairs?

Active listening involves giving our full attention to someone in an open, non-judgmental way. It involves focusing only on what that person is conveying to us in verbal and non-verbal language and feeding back in empathic phrases only what we feel the speaker's message meant - nothing more, nothing less.

Active listening allows the speaker to freely express her feelings because a non-judgmental, empathic response provides acceptance and warmth in the relationship. People become less afraid of their feelings when given the opportunity to discuss them openly.

The analysis of listening skills that follows is excerpted from "The Art of Listening" by Dominick A. Barbara.

Creative Listening

Creative listening is a process that is neither passive nor impositional; the listener's primary function is to encourage an attitude of self-examination and exploration. The listener's job is to assist the caller in recognizing the realities of the situation she confronts, and to explore the strategies open to her in resolving the problem. This art, like every art, must be developed by practice and skill.

Serious listening is total concentration on what is being received, plus awareness of the known facts. A good listener listens between the lines to the non-verbal meaning of the message. Patience must be practiced in the development of this skill. We are accustomed to doing many things at the same time (i.e. watching TV, reading, talking, smoking, eating). It seems we fear being alone, facing ourselves, defining ourselves, knowing ourselves, and have therefore almost destroyed our ability to perform effectively as a listener. Trained to believe we should be "people of action", we must now completely revamp our habits to become effective listeners.

*In the chapters that follow, I will be using feminine pronouns for ease of reading. It is meant to be inclusive of all people of both genders.

Learning to Listen to Ourselves

To fully concentrate, all distractions must be removed. We can then be alone with our innermost thoughts and feelings, and give ourselves and surroundings our whole interest and attention. At the same time we will be curious and alert. We will learn to live fully in the present and to evaluate things as they are, which will entail less time for trivial talk and more time for serious exchange of ideas, feelings and opinions.

Learning to Listen to Others

Good listening demands active participation and a good listener is curious and eager. The effective listener is constantly on the alert to find something interesting in what is said and attempts to keep the discussion moving and alive either by asking productive questions or by adding something constructive to the conversation. She times her responses so the receiver is capable of perceiving and interpreting them without undue difficulty or haste. The language used must be clear, concise, simple, and flexible.

As we communicate with each other in thoughtful, truthful meaning, a sense of responsibility, mutual rapport, and understanding will develop and grow. The aim of real communication is a " ...kind of communion with the other person, a sharing of one's self, and appreciation for the other which affirms the integrity of each ... ". Acceptance is the beginning. A developing communion and awareness of the other person follows. As we relax, we come closest to our feelings, and arrive at free verbal exchange when productivity reaches its highest peak; our listening becomes highly selective; and we become more aware and attuned to the essence of the facts or situation at hand. People have a drive toward self-realization which cannot be developed unless they are truthful to themselves and others in the spirit of mutuality, are active and productive, and relate to others.

Comprehension

An important factor in good listening is comprehension, the understanding and grasp of the true idea or meaning of what is heard. It involves the ability to recall immediately, or some time later, a sampling of what is being said or heard. This is difficult because we think faster than we talk. We speak at about 125 words per minute, and think four times that fast. It is what we do with this extra time that makes us good or poor listeners.

A poor listener becomes impatient, turns her thoughts to something else, comes back to the speaker, then loses the context of the conversation and finally gives up completely trying to understand or to listen.

A good listener is selective and uses her spare time in asking herself what is being said, in what context it is being said, and how accurate the facts are. She tries to be alone as much as possible with her own thoughts and feelings so that she can concentrate and listen with as little prejudice, condemnation, or criticism as possible. She makes a genuine effort to reach beyond the actual words that are spoken and get the basic meaning by visualizing the situation as a whole, remembering that different words mean different things to different speakers.

Emotional tones and attitudes color communication. In listening with arrogance or prejudice, the intent of the speaker is distorted. We must make a sincere effort to be open-minded and, to some degree, enter into the emotional life of the speaker. Information between two people can have context only when both the speaker and listener can reach levels of agreement regarding the statement of the subject matter at hand. Correct evaluation of the past and appropriate decisions for the future are largely based upon the relevance, accuracy and completeness of such information.

Need to Communicate

Severe mental depression is often noted among the hearing impaired. Our auditory sphere is one of our most sensitive ones, and one that connects a person to her environment more than any other. Our ears play a double role as a receiver of sound and a perceiver of words and situations. Our urge to communicate is to reveal ourselves and identify with others. This is the way we find real contact with the world around us. It may be that a lack of communication has largely, or certainly partially, caused the breakdown and confusion in our world today. This is certainly reflected in our youth. Actual records of crisis center calls throughout the world almost always reflect a breakdown of communication in the caller's life. Somewhere along the line, there has been a failure, either with parents, school, some other "establishment", or peers.

Positive Listening

It is essential for true emotional growth to be both heard and understood. A good listener gives the caller a chance to hear herself. She offers an empathic, understanding ear into which difficulties can be poured. In the strictest sense, people talk to hear themselves. It is by verbalizing that we can realize our innermost thoughts and problems. Often verbalizing alone can make an individual aware of the solution. By hearing oneself, vision and insight are possible. The closer a person is to herself and the more energies directed toward health and away from neurosis, the more realistic picture she will have of life and its problems.

Speech is called a "joint game between talker and listener against the forces of confusion". Tact, tolerance and consideration must be part of the effective communication process. Parents who don't listen to their children in the proper manner produce disturbed children. Too often we only hear and experience what interests us or stimulates our inner feelings. We place too much emphasis on the spoken word and too little on the non-verbal message.

Ineffective Listening

A logical or too intellectual person makes a poor listener. She listens only to what she expects to hear, blotting out reality. Vanity and egocentricity compel her to think solely of self. She generally fears close relationships and neglects the emotional non-verbal aspect of living.

An overly emotional or anxious person makes an equally poor listener. Communication is jammed with tension and excitement. Being afraid of conflict, the listener uses all her creative energies to avoid conflict and consequently has none left over for constructive use.

A rebellious listener is equally ineffective. She listens in a defensive and annoying manner. She is rarely enthusiastic about what is heard, is impatient, and interrupts at regular intervals. She must be in charge of the situation and have the last word. Her own egocentricity compels her to quote herself continuously and to make numerous personal references about her world, ideas and beliefs - all to the exclusion of anyone else's. The rebellious person regards the communicative situation chiefly as an arena for combat and intellectual survival.

Many people do not want to understand others or to be understood. They only want a superficial coating of external stimuli - answers to their own questions - and possess little insight, growth, or understanding. It is this kind of empty communication that leads to the scarcity of human contact in the world.

We must guard against being compulsive listeners. We must question our pre-conceived notions and attitudes toward others that color situations. The true meaning of a message is the personal translation between speaker and listener. There is almost always a difference, however slight, in the actual meaning between listener and speaker. A serious difference in meaning can block and prevent a trusted relationship from developing.

Listening is most effective when one is closest to being her real self. Those who wish to live in perpetual euphoria will fail. To be overly modest and self-effacing is a definite handicap. This person is at odds with herself and others. Her fear of facing facts of situations in their true perspectives makes her listen poorly and distort evaluations. To avoid anxiety and inner chaos, she manipulates the true meaning of messages and transforms them to satisfy her neurotic needs.

Pacing Ourselves

To listen with a purpose requires inner strength and the courage to open our minds to other people's ideas, while at the same time, facing up to the fact that some of our own beliefs may be inaccurate. Lack of courage prevents us from being flexible, empathetic, and willing to change. These attitudes must come from within. There must be empathy between speaker and listener, a feeling of one for another, and a deep sense of mutuality and respect. The good listener must believe herself before she can expect belief from others.

In the final process of growth, the last word must belong to the speaker. For the most part, the speaker can and will change when and if she understands the reasons why she should do so. By helping the speaker to be silent sometimes and listen to her own inner voice, the listener directs her toward putting her own conflicts and inner tensions into words. This will aid by removing those obstacles which interfered with emotional growth by permitting her to free her verbalizations from hindering contradictions and confusions.

Silence

Actual living occurs initially silently within us. Whatever we think, feel, believe or do starts silently. Silence allows us to use our capacities to the fullest and thus gives the greatest opportunity for observation. The art of silence gives time to look first before speaking, to search deeply within ourselves, to reflect seriously, and thus to develop a true creative outlook.

Many of us are too anxious to speak or too eager to accept as true all we hear from others. Productive or reflective silence is a quality which all of us should encourage and develop within ourselves. In talking to each other with better understanding, and searching actively and constructively within ourselves for the truth about our actual limitations, as well as our real potentialities, we shall arrive at a realistic, dynamic and complete awareness of what is, and so then shall enter into a truthful and healthy pattern of existence.

It is often more important to recognize what speech conceals and what silence reveals. Listening to one's inner self is difficult because the voice is often distant, feeble and indistinct. Conflicting thoughts and ideas of a painful nature which need to be felt consciously are silenced by superficial rationalizations and find their expression in the form of fears, phobias, and anxieties. Through the constructive use of silence we weave stronger ties than words can possibly achieve.

We must search ourselves for our inner truths and listen with our hearts. Communication means understanding, and understanding comes from our capacity for real listening and intuitive feeling and respect for others.

Qualities Necessary for Effective Listening

In order to be effective as a listener, one must have one's own inner problems reasonably worked out, or at least be so aware of them that they will not interfere with relating constructively to others. The listener must have an inherent belief in an individual's ability to change and grow. She must above all be a human being with sympathy for those who struggle and suffer, and the wish to use every human attribute within herself toward expressing warmth, understanding, sincerity, and respect for the speaker's own wishes and rights.

Qualities of an Effective Listener

1.   Willingness to accept nonjudgmentally all the speaker is conveying.

2.   Paraphrasing what is heard and checking for accuracy (see tentafiers) with the speaker at intervals throughout the interaction.

3.   Ability to integrate the words, tone, attitude and body language of the speaker and point out any discrepancies being observed. (For example: Pounding a fist and shouting "I am NOT angry!".)

4.   Ability to pick up on and reflect significant things that are NOT being said. (For example: A battered woman avoiding talking about her bruises.)

5.   An awareness of how one's own personal issues may influence an interaction with another. (For example: The listener grew up in an alcoholic home and realizes she has little compassion and actual anger toward the speaker's alcoholic wife.) The ability to monitor and control feelings for what is being heard is essential if one is to be helpful.

6.   Ability to sincerely convey warmth, understanding, positive regard and respect for the speaker while encouraging growth and change for her.

7.   Understanding that a listener's best aid comes from helping people to help themselves. Not to rescue, but to guide and empower them so they have the satisfaction and dignity of problem-solving, which they can then use in future situations.

2. EMPATHY

Empathy. Webster defines it this way: "The action of understanding, being aware of, being sensitive to, and vicariously experiencing the feelings, thoughts, and experience of another...". This skill, which involves the selflessness of concern ONLY for the client, is the cornerstone of crisis intervention. The listener is not feeling sorry FOR the client (that's sympathy), but is feeling WITH the client. It is both an intuitive sense all people have and a skill to be learned and honed. Empathy works at building trust because by using it, we allow a client to be herself. It's a way of telling someone that it's okay to feel what she is feeling.

In order to utilize empathic skills effectively, one must concentrate intensely on both the verbal and non-verbal behavior of the speaker. Concentration leads to more accurate understanding of the individual, and fewer errors of perception and judgment result. Initially, you must concentrate on responding interchangeably with the speaker. If you are able to respond with accuracy to both the feelings and the content of the person's messages, you will then establish a relationship based on trust. If trust is not established early in the conversation, attempts to be helpful will be fruitless. The speaker may decide not to take the risk of expressing feelings to someone she doesn't trust.

An effective listener learns to label the speaker's feelings and to formulate empathic responses in a language that is understandable to the speaker. Avoid jargon that may leave the speaker feeling confused and/or ignorant. Note the speaker's level of articulation and respond accordingly. Always respond in a tone or level that is similar to the speaker's, unless the speaker is hysterical or agitated. In such cases, a calm tone of voice is the most effective response and helps to defuse the situation. Tone of voice and nonverbal expressions that are congruent with the speaker's communicate an experimental understanding on the part of the listener, which in turn leads to further expression of feelings by the speaker.

In addition to concentrating on what the speaker is expressing, the listener must also be aware of what is not being expressed: undercurrent or implied messages. Acknowledging and responding to significant omissions can be a means of expressing a high level of empathy by giving the speaker permission to openly discuss what may have been perceived as "unspeakable" thoughts or feelings. The listener must then be guided by these responses in formulating subsequent communication. In this way, the listener can evaluate the effectiveness of higher responses based on their impact on the speaker.

Finally, the listener needs to be aware of her own reactions to both the speaker and the presented problem situation. Recognition, understanding, acceptance and setting aside of one's own thoughts, feelings, and values is essential in maintaining a position of neutrality. This position, in turn, is the prerequisite to the effective helping relationship.

FORMULATING AN EMPATHIC RESPONSE

In many cases, feelings are not directly stated or expressed by the speaker. Many undercurrent feelings may be perceived by observing non-verbal behavior and attending to the overall manner in which the speaker presents the situation (i.e. rate of speech, inflection, tone, body language, eye contact, etc.). Because mixed messages may be given, (i.e. "I'm very angry", spoken in monotone), it is imperative to preface an empathic response with a tentafying word, which allows the reflection to be made provisionally. It is then the speaker's turn to confirm or correct your perception. If we are inaccurate in what we are sensing, and do not allow ourselves to be corrected, we will be listening in a framework of false assumptions. The basic formula consists of:

TENTAFIER + FEELING ADJECTIVE

+ SOURCE OF THE FEELING

("It sounds like you feel + angry

+ because you didn't get a raise.")

Below is a list of tentafiers. This list is by no means exhaustive. It is rather a starting point. It takes practice to make these statements become a natural part of our vocabulary. It is also necessary to utilize a variety of tentafiers to avoid sounding rehearsed or repetitious.

TENTAFIERS

It sounds like you feel...

It seems as though you're feeling...

What I think I hear you saying is you feel...

Could it be that you're feeling...

I guess I'm hearing that you feel...

What I'm picking up is that you feel...

I sense that you're feeling...

TENTAFIERS (Continued)

Let me see if I understand you - you feel...

I'm perceiving that you feel...

Correct me if I'm wrong, but I think you're feeling...

Could this be what's going on - you feel...

I'm not sure if this is accurate, but you

seem to be feeling...

You appear to be feeling...

As I hear it, you feel...

I get the impression that you feel...

It seems that you feel...

So, you're feeling...

And that made you feel...

I hear you feeling...

My hunch is you're feeling...

I wonder if you are feeling...

I can't tell if you feel..., or you feel...

I get the feeling that you...

I hear you saying that...

If I understand you right, you...

Let me see if I'm with you so far; you...

So what you're saying is...

..., Is that what you are saying?

My impression is..., does that fit?

Would it be accurate to say that you...?

I'm thinking that you...

I'm picking up...

Sounds like there is a wish in there...

The part I understand is...

Throughout the intervention you will be using empathic responses and, when necessary, open-ended questions. 'Open-ended" questions generally cannot be answered with a "yes" or "no", and encourage the client to speak. Some examples follow.

OPEN ENDED QUESTIONS

Could you tell me...?

I'm wondering if...?

Can you say more about...?

Have you thought about...?

Are you saying...?

What does that mean to you...?

What (How) is that for you...?

I don't quite get what you mean, is it...?

How do you view that...?

Can you expand on that idea...?

For example...?

Do you have a specific example in mind...?

When you feel that way...?

Are you feeling that way now...?

What sort of things can you learn from this...?

What was that last comment...?

How do you mean that...?

Would it be accurate to say...?

Could you describe that in more detail...?

The part that still isn't clear to me is...?

I'm not clear on what you mean by...?

BARRIERS TO COMMUNICATION

As important as it is to know what facilitates good communication, we must also learn what may cause a breakdown in the conversation and inadvertently end the intervention.

In our attempts to be helpful we may inadvertently set up barriers which bring the conversation to a halt. The speaker may suddenly feel she no longer trusts the listener, or that the listener isn't accepting or approving of what is being heard. For example, the following list includes ways in which the listener communicates unacceptance.

1. Ordering, commanding, or directing

2. Lecturing or giving logical arguments

3. Warning or threatening

4. Giving "oughts" or "shoulds"

5. Advising, offering solutions or suggestions - especially if it is unsolicited

6. Probing, interrogating, or cross-examining

14   *Learning to Listen*

Other barriers to communication may include those which imply judgment or shame.

1. Name-calling, labeling, or stereotyping

2. Criticizing or judging

3. Blaming or disagreeing

4. Analyzing, diagnosing, or interpreting the situation for the speaker

Sometimes in our own fumble for words, we minimize the importance or intensity of what the speaker is trying to convey.

1. Agreeing that their perception is correct without moving to empathic response

2. Citing only the positive things while ignoring the negative side

3. Falsely reassuring them that all will be well

4. Sympathizing or consoling without moving to empathic response

If the listener hears things that make her feel uncomfortable, she may actually avoid it altogether. The speaker is then left wishing she had never brought up the topic. Some ways listeners avoid are:

1. Distracting the speaker

2. Withdrawing from the conversation

3. Humor

4. Sarcasm

5. Diversion (change the subject)

If we expect to become empathic, active listeners, we need to avoid using these tactics and many others which leave the speaker feeling empty and unheard.

3. CRISIS INTERVENTION

The Chinese have two characters for the one word "crisis". One means "danger". The other means "opportunity". It is our job as listeners to acknowledge the dangers heard, and encourage the speaker to find the opportunities for growth and change.

Definition of Crisis Intervention

Students of psychology, social work, counseling, clergy, and other helping professions are generally taught the skills necessary to be helpful in long-term situations. In my years as a supervisor in a crisis center, I saw many of these professionals come to us as volunteers to learn the art of crisis intervention.

Crisis intervention is a separate entity and a valuable skill for anyone to learn. Everyone encounters life crises at one time or another, and your ability to support someone through it may be life-changing for them. How do we define a "crisis"? Gerald Caplan, a pioneer in the field of preventative psychiatry, said it best:

> *"Crisis is not an illness. Instead, it can be defined as a time-limited period of psychological disequilibrium which is precipitated by a sudden and significant change in an individual's environment. The change demands an internal and external adjustment and expression. During this adjustment time, the person is often rendered incapable of self-mobilization."*

The key words in this definition are "time-limited". By this we mean that the situation can be generally resolved within about six weeks. It is always preceded by a "precipitating event" which triggers the state of disequilibrium to which Caplan refers.

For this discussion, we begin with a person who is in a balanced state of equilibrium emotionally, although those who are more unstable are certainly not immune. The steps that follow delineate the process of a crisis as it occurs. (Throughout this book the word "speaker" refers to the client/crisis bearer, while the term "listener" refers to you, the counselor/interventionist.)

Precipitating Event: Something happens which throws the person off-balance, and she finds that her usual coping skills are ineffective. This may be a break-up in a relationship, a death, a lost job, etc. <u>The event always involves LOSS, real or perceived, or the threat of loss.</u>

State of Disequilibrium: This may manifest itself in a number of ways. It may be felt as severe anxiety and/or tension. The person realizes that her coping skills aren't working, which in turn can lead to depression.

Recognition of Need to Reduce Stress: This recognition may be made by the crisis bearer, but is often noticed first by people close to them. This is when the person is at a critical turning point.

With proper support from a well-trained listener, the crisis bearer can be expected to return to her pre-crisis state of equilibrium within four to six weeks. Without support, the anxiety can escalate and compound into longer term dysfunctional behavior. Learning positive coping skills in this situation allows her to better deal with similar events in the future.

People in crisis are highly accessible emotionally because they want help with their pain, confusion, anxiety, etc. Your support is readily accepted, and your assurance that crisis is a normal, although unpredictable aspect of human growth, begins the process of normalizing their feelings. It is precisely because a crisis bearer is so suggestible that your skills need to be at their best if you are to be truly helpful.

Next, then, we will look at the nature of crisis intervention. Once these attributes are understood, we will move on to a simple eight step model which will become the framework for <u>every</u> intervention you will ever face.

Features of Crisis Intervention

The following features are characteristic of a well-managed crisis intervention.

Short Term: Generally, the pre-crisis equilibrium is restored within four to six weeks. When this is not accomplished, the client is advised that longer term help is needed, and appropriate referrals and follow-up are <u>always</u> given.

Non-Judgmental: As a listener we accept all that we hear without criticism or judgment. The client is trusting us with her feelings, and we are there to be empathic and supportive. We do not impose our feelings or disapprove of what we hear.

Focus on the Present: Because this anxiety was brought on by a recent event, our task is to keep the focus on the here and now. Talking about many past issues usually is best left to long-term therapists. We are attempting to help with <u>current</u> anxiety and situations.

Non-Directive: A person in crisis is highly suggestible because she wants the anxiety to end, and because she may consider the listener to be an "expert". Often she may ask for advice or inquire, "What would you do?" The well-trained listener will never tell her what to do. The task is to encourage her to seek and take responsibility for her own decisions. The listener facilitates this by exploring and clarifying the situation, and helping the client see her alternatives and their outcomes. (This is discussed at greater length in the section on the eight step model.)

Recognizes and Reinforces the Individual's Strengths:
It is not uncommon for a person in crisis to completely lose sight of all the coping mechanisms she possesses. A heightened sense of anxiety may make her feel out of control. The listener, therefore, must seek out and reflect those strengths to the client. In so doing, a client often becomes visibly relieved, and begins the process of restoring her own equilibrium. These reminders of her strengths are, in and of themselves, strength-building.

Differences Between Crisis Intervention and Therapy

The table on the following page outlines the differences between psychoanalysis, brief psychotherapy, and crisis intervention methodology.

MAJOR DIFFERENCES BETWEEN PSYCHOANALYSIS, BRIEF PSYCHOTHERAPY, AND CRISIS INTERVENTION METHODOLOGY

From: Crisis Intervention: Theory and Methodology, Aguioera and Messick, 2nd Edition, C.V. Mosby Company, Saint Louis, 1974.

	Psychoanalysis	Brief Psychotherapy	Crisis Intervention
Goal of Therapy	Restructuring the personality	Removal of specific symptoms	Resolution of immediate crisis
Focus of Treatment	1. Past unresolved issues 2. Freeing the unconscious	1. Past as it relates to present 2. Repression of unconscious and restraining drives	1. Present (Here and now) 2. Restoration to level of functioning prior to crisis
Usual activity of therapist	Passive observer	Participant observer	Active participant
Indications	Neurotic personality patterns	Acutely disruptive emotional pain and severely disruptive circumstances	Sudden loss of ability to cope with a live situation
Average length of treatment	Indefinite	From one to twenty sessions	From one to six sessions

THE PROCESS

In the crisis center where I worked, volunteers answered the crisis phones. The volunteers are screened into the program on the basis of several qualities such as warmth, sincerity, non-judgmental attitude, and the ability to learn and utilize good listening skills. Background/profession makes no difference. The 8-step model is the foundation for all interventions, and is outlined in this book. During the course of their 80 hour training, this model is practiced over and over and over again. The participants break into small groups in which one person is elected or volunteers to be the "crisis bearer". The story she tells may be real or contrived. The "interventionists" use the model to hone their skills before being allowed to take real phone calls. Phone calls are monitored by the supervisor until the trainees demonstrate their knowledge and skill in utilizing these newly learned techniques. A copy of the 8 steps is kept nearby for quick reference.

Once the volunteer becomes proficient with the model, the next step is to sit in with an experienced counselor for a face-to-face contact with a client. New insights are acquired in these sessions. Perhaps the best way to explain this is to break it down into two lists:

Verbal and Non-Verbal Signals
(What to Watch and Listen For)

Phone (voice only)	Face to Face	
Volume	Volume	Posture
Tension	Tension	Body Movements
Speed	Speed	Self-care (hygiene)
Stuttering	Stuttering	Eye contact (or lack of)
Silences	Silences	Facial Expressions
Crying	Crying	Body Language
Pitch	Pitch	Degree of Tension
Inflection	Inflection	Gestures

Communication is 7% words, 43% tone and 50% body and facial language. Obviously you are able to make an assessment quicker in person because of all the added signals you pick up. But a thorough assessment is possible on the phone as you learn to listen to vocal cues as well as background noise. Is the caller denying drinking as you hear ice cubes in a glass? Does the caller claim to be alone, yet you hear background voices? Is that another person or perhaps the TV? Is someone screaming at the caller? Is the caller safe?

For ease of reference, the eight step model of crisis intervention is outlined here. This is the concise form to be memorized and utilized in <u>every</u> intervention. It is followed by a step-by-step elaboration. It is extremely important to know that you must **never skip any of the steps**, although you may use them out of sequence at times. This is acceptable as long as all steps are used. It may be helpful to keep a copy of these steps near the phone until you become proficient.

You must also know that calls which appear to be "information only" are sometimes crisis calls. For example, a man may call asking if you have phone numbers for subsidized housing. These types of calls must <u>always</u> be explored before giving referrals. Perhaps he was just evicted. Maybe his wife asked him to leave. Maybe he is seeking information for a friend. He might be a therapist who needs referrals for a client. Because of the endless possibilities it is best to EXPLORE, EXPLORE, EXPLORE!

THE EIGHT STEP MODEL

1. Establish Trust and Rapport.

2. Explore and Clarify Entire Set of Circumstances, Including Support Systems.

3. Clarify Primary Problem and Prioritize Others.

4. Explore Past Problem Solving Methods.

5. Cite Desired Resolution.

6. Consider Options and Outcomes.

7. Decide on Precise Steps Necessary to Accomplish Goals.

8. Closure:

      A. Identify Next Move.

      B. Appointment, Referral, Follow-Up.

THE MODEL

STEP 1: ESTABLISH TRUST AND RAPPORT

How you relate to the client in the first few minutes sets the tone for the entire intervention. Your greeting must be warm and open and it must convey sincere interest in the client's welfare. Usually this process begins by introducing yourself and asking 'What's going on?" or more specifically, "Did something happen today?".

In these first few minutes you must also establish if this is an emergency situation. This is generally defined as a BLEEDING or BREATHING crisis. Has the client done anything to hurt herself? (Cut herself?, Overdosed?) Has she been physically abused? If this is a phone contact, you must also determine if the caller is safe now. If she is not safe where she is, the FIRST priority is to get her to a safe place. All else can wait if she is in physical danger. How you facilitate this depends on the policies of the agency for which you work. It may be sending the police. It may be sending a cab to bring her to your agency. However it is accomplished, it must be done FIRST.

In this first step you are able to assess the client's affect. Is she feeling angry? Frightened? Sad? Hopeless? As you begin to explore the precipitating event (What happened to initiate this contact?) you will begin to see which of three general categories this situation falls into: Is this a..

1. Situational Crisis - Did something happen recently, usually unexpectedly, to cause the person to experience a state of emotional disequilibrium? (i.e. - a death, sudden loss of a job, diagnosed with a chronic illness, etc.)

2. Developmental Crisis - This is sometimes referred to an "age/stage" crisis, and includes events such as retirement, grown children leaving home ("empty nest syndrome") or other life style changes that occur as a result of life's journey.

3. On-Going Pattern of Behavior - Usually the client has been struggling with the issue for some time, and this is most easily recognized to the listener as an "on-going" problem by the fact that there is no recent precipitating event. Often times, the client is in therapy and may become a recognized chronic caller. These clients must be confronted as frequent callers and usually be referred back to their therapists (unless there is a legitimate crisis to deal with) as soon as the caller is recognized. If the caller has no therapist, the interventionist can point out the long-term nature of the problem and give appropriate referrals.

STEP 2: EXPLORE AND CLARIFY ENTIRE SET OF CIRCUMSTANCES, INCLUDING SUPPORT SYSTEMS

This is the longest step of the model, when you will hear the details that led the client to contacting you. It takes a great deal of time because although we think 400-500 words per minute, we speak only 100-150. Let's say the caller tells you she lost her job. She is crying and screaming about how unfair this is. Your calm tone of voice and assurance that she can take her time in telling you will help defuse her. Empathic statements such as "I hear how angry and hurt you are feeling" will let her know you understand how she feels, and will encourage her to continue.

During the information gathering process it may become necessary to ask questions. Questions should be kept to a minimum at this stage though, because they can be detracting to the flow of an interaction and tend to keep the speaker away from her feelings. They should be used only for clarification. Most of the time, however, clarification and additional information may be obtained through reflective responses. When this is not successful, open and indirect questions are the most useful. Avoid questions that may be answered with a "yes" or "no". Open and indirect questions invite the speaker to give more information. It is more like making a statement that implies a question than a direct query. (You will find a list on page 12.) Too many questions, however, may leave the speaker feeling as though she is being interrogated. When an issue has been clarified, it is best to revert back to empathic responses. Appropriate questions at this point would be "When did this happen?" and "Could you tell me the reason you lost your job?".

As she answers your questions you will again utilize empathic responses. You will label and reflect stated or obvious feelings as well as undercurrent ones you are sensing. These empathic statements must ALWAYS begin with a TENTAFIER. This is a phrase that tentatively states what you think you heard, and allows the client the opportunity to confirm or correct your statement. It also tells the client you have been actively listening to her. (A list of tentafiers and a formula for empathic response appear on page 10.)

During this process you will also be alert to verbal and non-verbal clues the client is exhibiting. These include, but are not limited to voice tone, pitch, tension, speed, silences, stuttering or crying if the client is on the phone. In person you would also be aware of posture, facial expressions, gestures, eye contact (or lack of), body movements, and degree of tension.

The whole purpose of this step is to increase the understanding of the problem situation. Problem-solving can wait until you both have a clearer picture of the circumstances.

For example, during the course of this process, the caller relates that she lost her job due to excessive drinking which caused poor work performance. She tells you her drinking increased a few months ago when she discovered her husband was having an affair. Her teenage son has been acting out, and was recently suspended from school for fighting in gym class. Her bills are piling up and she is beginning to feel hopeless. Throughout all this you are utilizing empathic responses.

When all the issues have been named, you will need to find out how the client is hoping you can be helpful. This question must be asked gently and sincerely. The reason to ask this is to find out if the client's expectations fall within the parameters of aid you or your agency can offer. For example, if this caller's response to "How are you hoping we can help you today?" is "I'm hoping you'll call my boss and explain all the stress I'm feeling, and ask him to give me another chance", you can inform her of your policies regarding that. If that is something you can't do, she needs to know that now, so other alternatives can be explored. The point here is not to end the intervention, but rather to keep her realistic in her hopes. It's much better to clarify your limitations early in the contact so other options can be explored. (Options are explored most thoroughly in Step 6.) Once you and the client feel certain that all the issues have been named, it's time to move on to Step 3.

STEP 3: CLARIFY PRIMARY PROBLEM AND PRIORITIZE OTHERS

In this step you will review (by using reflective statements) the various issues cited in Step 2. It is now time to focus on clarifying one issue at a time, and find out which issue is of primary importance to the client. (This is not always the first issue she presented.) You may ask something like "What do you see as the biggest issue in all this?" It is important to remember that your opinion of what is most important doesn't matter. The client must identify what she sees as most troubling, because these are the issues she will be most willing to work on. Your task is to help her prioritize the problems specifically. This compartmentalization allows the speaker a chance to view each matter individually, and she begins to feel less overwhelmed. Be aware of your own feelings and reactions in this step, too, as your view of the priorities may differ greatly from hers.

For example, the caller may say her first priority is getting back to work so she can pay bills. Perhaps you feel she needs help with the drinking before anything can change for her. You can present the thought to her using a reflection and an open-ended question such as "You told me that your drinking cost you your last job. Have you thought about seeking treatment before tackling any of the other issues?" Maybe she hasn't thought of that. Or maybe she isn't ready to seek treatment. It will always be up to her to decide what needs attention first. You can discover what it is by stating something like "You have been talking about several issues. Which one is most important to you?"

Once that question is answered, you can begin the process of prioritizing the issues. Remember that you will explore solutions to the problems in detail in steps 6 and 7. The task here is to list the problems in order of importance to the client.

Let's say she decides that she needs to seek help with her alcohol problem first. She thinks this will better enable her to work on her marriage and find a job. She feels her son's behavior will improve as a result of her sobriety, and a new job will help pay the bills. So, if we were to make a list, it would look like this:

1. Quit Drinking

2. Deal with Marriage Issues

3. Attend to Son's Behavior Problems

4. Find a Job

5. Pay Off Bills

Having a clear picture of this, it's time to move on to Step 4.

STEP 4: EXPLORE PAST PROBLEM-SOLVING METHODS

Now that you have reviewed and prioritized the problems, you will help the client look back at her problem-solving techniques in the past. Your questions will be designed to help her see whether or not her past skills worked then, and whether they will work now.

Appropriate questions here are: "Have you been in a similar situation before?" If so, "What did you do then?" "Did it work?" "Will it work now?" "If not, WHY not?"

You also need to find out how the client feels about solving the problem. For example, she may be afraid of quitting her drinking. She may be feeling ambivalent about "saving" her marriage. She may feel resentful of having to find a job. She may feel angry about her son's rebellious behavior. She is probably anxious over her mounting debt. All of these feelings need to be acknowledged and dealt with using empathic response. Her feelings toward the problems play a major role in how she will choose to handle (or avoid) them.

It is your job as the listener to identify ways you see the client avoiding solving a problem, too. For example, you may see her shifting uncomfortably each time the topic turns to paying the bills. She may dismiss it as something that will take care of itself when she finds a job. But problems do not take care of themselves, and you must help her acknowledge that. Once it is looked at, the road to finding a solution is made clearer.

If the client's past problem-solving methods worked before, perhaps she needs only to discuss them, and reinforcement from you will help strengthen her to try it again. If her methods failed or she hasn't been faced with these issues before, your guidance in helping her find solutions that will see her through is invaluable. You are also helping her to find strength for future problem-solving if and when she is faced with similar problems. She will have learned new coping skills.

STEP 5: CITE DESIRED RESOLUTION

Step 5 involves finding out what the client hopes will happen. Appropriate questions could be:

"What would you like to see happen?"
"How are you hoping this will all turn out?"

By naming her expectations, she is setting the stage for task delineation. As she specifies her hopes, she will begin to clarify in her own mind what she must do next. You will explore options and tasks in Steps 6 and 7. For the moment, you are only trying to help her see what the end result will look like. Only in this way can she begin to see what steps need to be taken to get there.

For example, our client may answer your question by saying that she would like to quit drinking for good. She may also like to get her family involved in counseling, clear up her debts and find a job training program to learn new skills.

Now that she has stated what she hopes to accomplish, it is time to move to Step 6.

STEP 6: CONSIDER OPTIONS AND OUTCOMES

This step can be thought of as the "What if...?" step. It is now time to brainstorm with the client.

In the last step, she told you what she would like to see happen. Let's look at one of her resolutions in the context of "What if...?"

She wants to stop drinking permanently. She feels that her drinking is not frequent enough to require inpatient detoxification. Options to examine might include:

"What if you tried stopping on your own?"
"How do you think an outpatient program would be helpful?"
"How do you feel about attending AA meetings?"

The idea here is to get as many ideas on the table as the two of you can.

Then the possible outcomes must be considered. The conversation may sound something like this:

CLIENT: "I think I can stop drinking on my own."

LISTENER: "What would you do if that doesn't work?"

CLIENT: "I guess I could try AA meetings."

LISTENER: "And if that didn't feel like enough support?"

CLIENT: "Then I suppose I'd try to find a more structured outpatient program."

And so it goes with each of her desired resolutions. Maybe her husband and son will refuse to go to a therapist with her. What then? Will she go alone? Will she not go at all? Has she considered divorce? Could she call her creditors and make payment arrangements? What about filing for bankruptcy? What can she do if they refuse to work with her? Is she willing to look into job training programs? Has she thought about going back to school? How does she feel about it? What will she do if her plan doesn't work? Be certain to build in a contingency plan so she is less likely to feel defeated if her plan fails.

Remember to use open-ended questions which encourage conversation. You want the client to explore all alternatives and their consequences. This is the time to again reinforce the client's strengths, especially for her problem-solving efforts.

Once the client feels satisfied that all her choices have been discussed, you can move to Step 7.

STEP 7: DECIDE ON PRECISE STEPS NECESSARY TO ACCOMPLISH GOALS

At this point it is time to discuss the client's plan in detail. You will assist the client in outlining specifically the tasks which are needed to effect change. This empowers her to help herself rather than having someone do it FOR her. Specific tasks can stabilize someone who feels overwhelmed by many issues. She needs to prioritize her choices.

So the outline your client decides on may look like this:

1. Call AA and plan to attend a meeting.

2. Accept referrals from you for a family therapist.

3. Call creditors to discuss financing.

4. Go to library to find information on local job training programs.

It is your job to summarize and clarify all her decisions. You will very specifically reflect her needed actions and have her include a time frame for implementation of them. By now she will have gained some sense of control, and her anxiety will begin to ease.

STEP 8: CLOSURE

A. Identify Next Move
B. Appointment, Referral, Follow-Up

How will the client begin to implement her chosen course of action? What will she do today after your conversation with her ends?

There are two considerations in this step:

1. What will she do for herself?

2. What will your role be in following up with her?

The plan needs to be very specific in naming the tasks she must do. Perhaps our client will tell you she plans to go home and call AA. She intends to go to a meeting today. She will make an appointment with the family therapist you gave her as a referral. She will gather up her bills this week and review them before calling creditors to arrange payment. She may have to call a credit counselor to educate herself and/or utilize their services. She feels better just knowing she is capable of doing these things herself, and doing them effects change.

Your role in following up with the client depends on the policy of your agency. Perhaps it will mean another meeting or phone call with her next week to see how she's feeling and what she may have accomplished thus far. In the agency where I worked we generally limited our services to six visits. However, if you encounter a problem with a client that is beyond your agency's capability, it is appropriate (and practically imperative) to refer the client (at the end of the first intervention) to a suitable therapist or service. You are helping the client far more in this way than you would by allowing her to erroneously believe you can be of help to her.

However this closure is handled, it is important to NEVER leave the client feeling you are saying "Good luck!" and offering nothing else. Knowing you care what happens to her gives her a sense of accountability that may help motivate her to accomplish her tasks.

4. SUICIDE

"Suicide is NOT a crisis."

At first glance, this statement seems to be a contradiction in terms. But it is one of the most important things to remember when you encounter a person who is feeling suicidal.

Suicide is not a crisis. It is the person's perceived solution to a crisis.

Suicide is a permanent solution to temporary problems. The task of the interventionist is to help the person identify and deal with the underlying problems. How is this accomplished? It is accomplished using the very same 8-step model used for every crisis intervention.

Suicidal ideation may or may not be verbalized by the crisis bearer. It is not always easy to tell if a client is feeling suicidal if she doesn't come right out and say it. But there are some clues in the conversation that will cause you to suspect it. She may say things like: "They'd be better off without me." or "I won't be around much longer anyway." or "It won't matter soon." or "I won't be here by then." The moment you suspect suicidal thoughts you must ASK the client about it. You will NOT plant the idea in her head - she already knows, however fleeting the thought, that it is an option. You must ask because in so doing, you give her permission to discuss it and normalize her feelings. Appropriate questions are: "Are you feeling suicidal?" or "Have you been thinking about suicide?". If the answer is "no", you continue with the intervention as before.

If, however, the answer is "yes", you now have many things to explore. The first question is "Have you thought about **HOW** you would kill yourself?" This question may sound harsh, but know that this is not the time for flowery language or euphemisms. Your words must be based in the reality that the client is talking about death. The answer to this is your first step in assessing the lethality of your client. If she shrugs and says "I don't know" she is somewhat less lethal than if she says "I plan to overdose on sleeping pills Thursday night." If she plans to overdose, your next question is "Do you have a bottle of sleeping pills?" Again, lethality is much higher if she has the means to do it.

Next you will find out if she has made any previous gestures or attempts. (Obviously if an attempt is currently underway (i.e. took pills before calling) you treat it as a medical emergency and deal with issues later.) A 'gesture' may be taking a less than lethal overdose or cutting one's self superficially. This is the type of thing that many people around the client don't take seriously. Maybe she's done it a number of times before. You may hear others say "She's only trying to get attention." Indeed she **is** trying to get attention - attention that she desperately NEEDS. It's ludicrous how so many people use this profoundly true statement to rationalize their decision to totally ignore the situation. An 'attempt' is generally considered to be a near-lethal experience. Every gesture or attempt, regardless of how numerous, needs to be taken seriously. Each successive attempt increases the likelihood of succeeding the next time.

You will also ask if there is any family history of suicide. Although there is no genetic tendency for suicide, it occurs more frequently in families because it is seen and learned as a coping mechanism. This is also true in peer groups, especially among teenagers. In a local high school where a suicide occurred, it was followed by six more in the ensuing two years. This is a very important component in assessing lethality.

Once you have learned these things, you will have a good concept of how lethal the person is. But we're not done yet. Now is the time to discuss death. Getting the client talking about it makes it more real to her. What are her beliefs about death? How will her death impact others? A common knee-jerk answer to this is "They won't care." Exploring this will often result in her seeing that people will care. Or you may hear, "They'll get over it." No they won't - not completely. A suicide is life-altering for the survivors. Speaking graphically about suicide is acceptable because the finality of this choice must be realized by the client. What will the death scene look like? Who will find you? How will that be for them?

A "no-suicide contract" is always attempted in interventions involving a suicidal person. This consists of asking the person to promise not to do anything to harm herself without first contacting someone with whom she can discuss it. This may be a verbal or written contract, and those who agree to it overwhelmingly abide by it. One reason this works so well is the client now knows somebody cares. You have conveyed that throughout the intervention.

The ultimate responsibility in making the decision to live or die lies only with the client, and you need to know and believe that completely if you are to be an effective interventionist. If you don't realize this, you will probably suffer from burnout in a very short period of time.

THIRD PARTY INTERVENTIONS

Occasionally you may get a call from someone who knows someone who is feeling suicidal. She is calling to get advice. She doesn't know what to do.

A person in this position does bear a <u>LIMITED</u> amount of responsibility toward the suicidal person. Offering support is the essential element and this can be accomplished in a number of ways. The caller may respond to her friend in the following ways:

1.   Recognizing and responding to suicidal clues and messages frees the person to discuss her feelings. A nonjudgmental attitude and the assurance that you take her seriously is imperative. Accept her feelings and encourage her to talk.

2.   Do not minimize or discount what she is saying. A failing grade or lost job may seem trivial to you, but if she is saying it is enough to make her want to kill herself, <u>believe her</u>. <u>Your</u> thoughts on their significance have no place here.

3.   Tell her what she means to you. She may be feeling that she isn't important to anyone - that no one will care if she dies.

4.   Help her to consider alternatives. Brainstorm with her about possible resolutions to the problem she is presenting.

5.   Don't leave her alone if you believe she will attempt suicide in the near future. Offer to take her to a crisis center or emergency room.

6.   Involve others. The more people that know about this, the better chance that she will feel loved. Family, friends, clergy, teachers, and therapist may all be in a position to help. You must not promise to keep this secret. If this promise has already been made, break it. It's too big a responsibility for one person to feel, especially if she dies.

7.   Ask her to make a 'no-suicide contract' with you. This is a promise from her that she will not harm herself without calling you (or a crisis center, emergency room, pastor, etc.) first.

8.   Most importantly, you must know that the ultimate responsibility and decision is <u>HERS</u>, not yours. You can be supportive and offer to assist in getting professional help, but the final decision rests with <u>HER</u>.

The four tables on the following pages are reprinted by permission of the Neighborhood Service Organization-Emergency Telephone Service/Suicide Prevention Center; Detroit, Michigan. They will be found to be valuable in understanding, evaluating and dealing with the issue of suicide. This author's gratitude is extended.

INDICATORS OF LETHALITY
(An Individual's Potential for Suicide)

Emotional State: i.e., Severely depressed, extremely out of control, affect that is flat or inappropriate. Remember that extremes are dangerous.

Suicide Plan: Look at availability, lethality, and specificity of plan, remembering that the greater any of these factors, the more lethal the threat.

Prior Suicide Attempts: This is considered the best single indicator of lethality.

Recent Loss: (i.e., loved one, job, etc.) Remember that the importance of the loss is what it means to the individual.

Medical Problems: Especially anything physically debilitating.

Resource Ring: Who is available to the individual? How willing is that individual to utilize his/her resources? How helpful does he/she perceive them to be? Were they willing to seek out resources when few or none already exist for them? Do you feel he/she will utilize them?

Life Messages: What people/things are important in the individual's daily life? (i.e., home, family, school, work, activities, hobbies, friendships, religion.) Does the individual have future plans?

Has a Friend or Family Member Committed Suicide?   If so, the individual is eight times more likely to attempt.

Substance Abuse: Alcohol and/or drug use increases lethality.

No Suicide Promise: Was the individual willing/reluctant/unwilling to give a no suicide promise?

The greater any of these factors the higher the lethality.

THE MYTHOLOGY OF SUICIDE

MYTH: If people talk about killing themselves, they won't really do it.

FACT: Talking about suicide is often a clue or warning of a person's intentions. Always take any mention of suicide seriously.

MYTH: Suicide tendencies are inherited.

FACT: Although several suicides can happen in one family, it appears to be a response to previous suicides, not a genetically transmitted one.

MYTH: Suicidal people want to die - and feel there is no turning back.

FACT: Suicidal people usually want to get rid of their problems and emotional pain more than they do their lives.

MYTH: All suicidal people are deeply depressed.

FACT: This is often true, however, not always apparent. Some suicidal people appear to be happier than they have been, because they've decided to "resolve" all their problems through suicide.

MYTH: There is a low correlation between alcoholism and suicide.

FACT: Alcohol can have a trigger effect on suicidal people and is often ingested before the suicide by alcoholics and non-drinkers alike.

MYTH: Suicidal people are mentally ill.

FACT: Some mentally ill people do kill themselves, however, the majority of suicidal people are ordinary and seemingly healthy.

MYTH: Asking people if they are suicidal might plant the idea in their heads.

FACT: Asking people about suicidal intent will often lower the anxiety level and act as a deterrent to suicidal behavior by encouraging the ventilation of pent-up emotions.

MYTH: Suicide is more common among lower income groups.

FACT: Suicide crosses all social-economic boundaries and no one class is more susceptible than another.

MYTH: Professional people do not kill themselves.

FACT: Physicians, lawyers, dentists, and pharmacists appear to have high suicide rates.

MYTH: When a depression lifts, there is no longer any danger of suicide.

FACT: The greatest danger of suicide exists during the first three months after a person recovers from a deep depression. The reason they may be happier can come from their decision to die and end their pain.

MYTH: Suicide occurs without warning.

FACT: Most suicidal people plan their self-destruction in advance and then present clues indicating that they have become suicidal.

Neighborhood Service Organization-Emergency Telephone Service/Suicide Prevention Center - Detroit, Michigan

CLUES TO SUICIDE

1. Eating Problems - Either eating too much or too little.

2. Sleeping Problems - Sleeping too much or too little, waking up too early.

3. Social Withdrawal

   a. Less participation in classes.
   b. Dropping out of extra curricular activities.
   c. Less "hanging out".
   d. Quitting part-time job.

4. Decrease in Self Care

   a. Appearance looks messier/school work is less carefully done.
   b. Increased tardiness and/or absence from school/work.
   c. Falling grades/work performance.

5. Emotional Behavior

   a. Crying easily or for no apparent reason.
   b. Rowdy behavior or physical fighting.
   c. Looking only at the negative/hopeless side of life or a focus on death.
   d. Verbal expressions such as "I can't take it anymore", "I just want to die", "You won't have to worry about me anymore", etc..
   e. Greater irritability and intolerance.
   f. Frequent daydreaming.
   g. Talking about joining someone who is already dead.

6. Getting Things in Order

   a. Accomplishing tasks previously put off (i.e. cleaning up room, getting haircut, catching up on homework).

   b. Giving away things - usually valued objects.

   c. Making plans to donate body.

   d. Paying debts/getting finances in order/taking out insurance policies.

  e. Visiting old friends/relatives - apologizing for old (often forgotten) arguments.

  f. Giving a note to a friend to give to a family member "in a couple of days".

  g. Circling or writing down songs or poems that talk about suicide, death, or afterlife.

  h. Arranging to have children or pets taken care of.

7. Increased Frequency of Drug (including alcohol) Abuse

8. Collecting pills, Buying a gun, etc...

9. Sudden, Dramatic Improvement After a Period of Depression/Serious Problems

10. Recent Loss

  a. Death (natural, accidental, suicide) of a family member or friend or anniversary of death.

  b. Failure at school or job.

  c. Health problems and complaints (i.e. frequent headaches, stomach aches, visits to school nurse).

  d. Break up of a relationship with boy or girl friend.

  e. Argument with parent/other family members or friends.

  f. Divorce of parents or self.

11. Previous Suicide Attempts/Family History of Suicide.

Neighborhood Service Organization-Emergency Telephone Service/Suicide Prevention Center - Detroit, Michigan

TIPS FOR SIGNIFICANT OTHERS

1. Do not hesitate to get involved. Whether you are a best friend or a passerby you could be the crucial person in saving a life. Have faith in your ability to do so.

2. Always take any mention of death or suicide, even a joke or off-hand comment seriously. Your concern will not plant the idea of suicide in a person's head. In fact, it may relieve a person's distress because you are taking them seriously.

3. NEVER keep information about someone being suicidal to yourself, even if that person has sworn you to confidence. Share a secret; save a friend.

4. Realize that people may vent their anger at you, and that it is still your responsibility to do everything you can to prevent them from killing themselves. They are in crisis and their judgment about their own wants and needs is not to be trusted. Chances are they want help and do not know how to ask any other way.

5. Do not say "time heals all wounds". Sometimes it does and sometimes it doesn't. Suicidal persons feel they have no time left.

6. Do not tell potentially suicidal people they are crazy or just trying to get attention. They may end up actually harming themselves to get the attention they need.

7. Do not tell a suicidal person to "go ahead and do it". The person already has many reasons for not wanting to live. Regardless of your intent, your suggestion may be received as an invitation.

8. Do not play amateur psychotherapist. Do all you can to get the person to a professional as quickly as possible. If you think they may kill themselves at any moment, call a suicide prevention center or go with them to an emergency room.

9. Do not discuss whether it would be better to live or die. Your attitude should be that you friend MUST live. He or she knows enough reason not to live.

10. Be supportive. Knowing that someone is concerned is vital to a person suffering depression.

11.   NEVER leave potentially suicidal people alone. Get them to agree not to hurt themselves before consulting you or preferably a professional. Help them locate a suicide prevention center or other 24 hour crisis phone number. This is usually available on the front page of the phone book.

12.   Do everything you can for the person. It is always worth a try. You may succeed in saving a life. Remember, however, you cannot take responsibility for the person's decision. Ultimately, that is his or her own choice.

Neighborhood Service Organization-Emergency Telephone Service/Suicide Prevention Center - Detroit, Michigan

5. "FEELINGS" VOCABULARY

ABANDONED

Synonym: Deserted, neglected, forsaken, forgotten, shunned, forlorn.

Ever since your last child moved away you've been feeling abandoned.

ABSORBED

Synonym: Swallowed up, preoccupied, consumed.

You seem to be feeling so totally absorbed in this problem that you can't even function normally.

ADAMANT

Synonym: Determined, fixed, resolute.

It sounds like you feel adamant that the school is not giving your child the support she needs.

ADRIFT

Synonym: Lost, floating, drifting.

They handed you an early retirement before you really wanted it and now you're feeling adrift.

ADULTERATED

Synonym: Infected, polluted, corrupted, contaminated, cheapened, devalued.

And that made you feel adulterated when he made those crude accusations.

AFFECTED

Synonym: Moved, touched, stirred, impressed.

So, you felt really affected by the small child's tears.

AFFECTIONATE

Synonym: Tender, loving, kind.

You seem to be feeling affectionate towards her, but she keeps pushing you away.

AFFLICTED

Synonym: Troubled, tormented, hurt.

I'm sensing that you're feeling afflicted by the letters from the IRS.

AFRAID

Synonym: Frightened, fearful, nervous, uneasy, intimidated.

I hear you saying that you're feeling afraid because you are getting these weird phone calls.

AGGRAVATED

Synonym: Annoyed, provoked, bothered.

So, you're feeling aggravated that the cop tried to blame the accident on you.

AGGRESSIVE

Synonym: Belligerent, combative,
                     hostile, offensive.

I hear you feeling aggressive toward
your boss when he shows so little
respect for people.

AGITATED

Synonym: Disturbed, upset,
                     stirred up, pissed off.

It seems that you feel very
agitated at your neighbor's
refusal to clean up his yard.

AGONIZING

Synonym: Suffering, struggling, tormenting.

It sounds like you're agonizing over your daughter's promiscuous
reputation.

AGREEABLE

Synonym: Cooperative, acceptable, pleasant.

So, you're feeling agreeable with our plan for a stay at a rehab
center.

ALARMED

Synonym: Scared, frightened, aroused.

When the counselor said your son might be doing drugs, you felt
alarmed at the suggestion.

ALIENATED

Synonym: Rejected, left out, unfriendly.

I wonder if you're feeling alienated because of the comments about your foreign car.

ALONE

Synonym: Lonely, deserted, forsaken, abandoned.

It sounds like you feel very alone since you've moved to this new town and can't seem to make new friends.

AMBIGUOUS

Synonym: Uncertain, vague, doubtful.

I'm sensing that you're feeling ambiguous about your future with her.

AMBITIOUS

Synonym: Energetic, hopeful, zealous, intent.

Now that you're retired you're really feeling ambitious, but your wife doesn't seem to want to do anything.

AMIABLE

Synonym: Pleasant, charming, friendly.

So, you were feeling amiable towards the officers, but they threw you up against the car anyway.

AMUSED

Synonym: Cheerful, entertained, humored.

You felt amused by the joke about your wife, but she didn't think it was so funny.

ANGRY

Synonym: Enraged, irate, furious, resentful,
             irritated, bitter, hateful, annoyed, provoked.

I hear that you were feeling angry when the boss turned down your idea.

ANGUISHED

Synonym: Distressed, hurt, tormented, tortured.

You've had your heart broken before and the thought of it happening again leaves you feeling anguished.

ANIMATED

Synonym: Lively, happy spirited, gay.

So, you were feeling quite animated as you performed at the karaoke bar.

ANIMOSITY

Synonym: Dislike, hatred, displeasure.

It's been fifteen years since the divorce but you still feel animosity towards him.

ANNIHILATED

Synonym: Demolished, exterminated, obliterated.

So, you felt annihilated by your boss's verbal attack in front of everyone.

ANNOYED

Synonym: Troubled, pestered, irritated.

It sounds like you feel annoyed at his constant chattering while you're trying to read.

ANONYMOUS

Synonym: Nameless, ignored, unacknowledged.

It sounds like you felt anonymous when no one in the group acknowledged you.

ANTAGONIZED

Synonym: Provoked, irritated, tortured.

Are you saying that you felt antagonized when everyone else got a raise?

ANXIOUS

Synonym: Troubled, concerned, apprehensive.

I'm hearing you say that you were feeling a bit anxious about giving the presentation to your peers.

APATHETIC

Synonym: Cold, unconcerned, unemotional.

I sense that the upcoming election leaves you feeling apathetic despite your social consciousness.

APOLOGETIC

Synonym: Regretful, sorry, remorseful.

So, you're feeling apologetic, but she won't even return your calls.

APPALLED

Synonym: Dismayed, shocked, horrified.

You felt appalled by the child's language, but his mother didn't even seem to notice.

APPEALING

Synonym: Attractive, enticing, alluring.

So, you're saying that you felt more appealing after he complemented you.

APPRECIATIVE

Synonym: Thankful, grateful, indebted, obliged.

You were feeling appreciative that the boys cleaned your yard and cut your lawn, but then they tried to extort all that money from you.

APPREHENSIVE

Synonym: Worried, troubled, fearful, uncertain.

It's been over twenty years since you last went to school and the thought of returning leaves you feeling apprehensive.

APPROACHABLE

Synonym: Sociable, agreeable, friendly, receptive, congenial.

It sounds like you felt approachable all evening, but still no one asked you to dance.

ARGUMENTATIVE

Synonym: Quarrelsome, contentious, pugnacious.

You always manage to make a fool of yourself when you're feeling so argumentative, and then later regret it.

ARROGANT

Synonym: Insolent, overbearing, aloof, egotistic, smug.

You say you felt arrogant when you flipped him off, stamped out and slammed the door, but now you're lost and alone.

ASHAMED

Synonym: Embarrassed, demeaned, debased, discomforted.

You've been caught shoplifting three times and you say you're feeling ashamed.

ASININE

Synonym: Stupid, foolish, silly, idiotic, simple, inane, insipid.

Now you feel asinine when you look back and realize how self-destructively you acted.

ASSAULTED

Synonym: Attacked, raped,
              violated, ravished.

You came in and found ·
someone had rifled your
desk while you were gone
and you feel assaulted.

ASSERTIVE

Synonym: Positive, confident, certain, absolute.

You were feeling assertive when you presented the idea, but everyone shot you down.

ASSURED

Synonym: Confident, persuaded, promised, convinced.

It sounds like you felt assured of a positive outcome in spite of the odds.

ASTONISHED

Synonym: Amazed, surprised, startled, shocked, bewildered.

It sounds like you felt astonished to find a bonus in your paycheck.

ASTOUNDED

Synonym: Shocked, startled, surprised, amazed.

You seem to feel astounded that you can trust again after all these years.

ATTENTIVE

Synonym: Mindful, observant.

So, you found it difficult to feel attentive in church with all the crying babies around you?

ATTRACTIVE

Synonym: Beautiful, charming, handsome, engaging.

You're saying you felt attractive when you went to the door, and his first comment was; "Hurry up and get ready".

AVID

Synonym: Eager, greedy, desirous, enthusiastic.

So, you felt avid about having the class reunion, and then didn't even go yourself.

AWESTRUCK

Synonym: Impressed, exalted, overwhelmed.

Just the sight of the Rocky Mountains leaves you feeling awestruck.

AWFUL

Synonym: Horrible, terrible, dreadful, disgusted, offensive, repulsive.

Being a witness to such a terrible accident has left you feeling awful.

AWKWARD

Synonym: Clumsy, not graceful, floundering, inept, unfit.

You're telling me you felt awkward when asked to do a role play for the group.

BAFFLED

Synonym: Perplexed, confused, puzzled, bewildered.

You felt baffled at the meeting when everyone got excited again about the same old ideas.

BAMBOOZLED

Synonym: Tricked, swindled, duped, deceived.

You paid $1200 for repairs, the problem hasn't been corrected, and you're feeling really bamboozled?

BANISHED

Synonym: Expelled, outcast, ostracized, dismissed, exiled, rejected.

It sounds like you felt banished when your friends went to the parity without you.

BATTERED

Synonym: Beaten, punished, mauled.

It seems like you feel battered every time he criticizes you.

BEASTLY

Synonym: Savage, disgusting, brutal, foul, gross, inhuman, vile, obscene.

It sounds like you felt beastly to learn that it was once rumored that your grandfather was a werewolf.

BEAUTIFUL

Synonym: Attractive, pretty, enticing, pleasing, lovely, charming, imposing, majestic.

It sounds like you feel beautiful every time he looks at you that way.

BECOMING

Synonym: Handsome, suitable, attractive, tasteful, agreeable.

You felt becoming in your new Easter hat, got to church, and no one was wearing hats.

BEFUDDLED

Synonym: Confused, doubtful, intoxicated, inebriated.

So, you felt befuddled by the professor's dialogue but tried to fake it anyway.

BEHOLDEN

Synonym: Obligated, indebted, responsible.

She stood by you so many times and you feel beholden, but you still just want to be left alone.

BELITTLED

Synonym: Lowered, humbled, disparaged.

You felt belittled when they told you that you were too short to be a cop.

BELLIGERENT

Synonym: Hostile, aggressive, pugnacious, warlike.

You're saying you felt belligerent when the broker pressured you, slammed down the phone, and now the stock is up 9 points in four days.

BELOVED

Synonym: Loved, adored, prized, cherished, treasured, revered, venerated.

It sounds like you felt beloved when your child held your hand in public.

BEMUSED

Synonym: Dazed, confused, muddled, bewildered.

You seem to be feeling bemused by your child's sudden change in behavior.

BENEFICENT

Synonym: Helpful, kind, benign, benevolent.

When you donate blood you feel beneficent, but are wondering if it's safe.

BENEVOLENT

Synonym: Generous, helpful, altruistic, kind.

It seems that doing volunteer work leaves you feeling benevolent.

BERATED

Synonym: Scolded, reprimanded, chided, rebuked.

It sounds like you felt berated when the judge rattled off all your traffic violations.

BERSERK

Synonym: Frenzied, crazed, raged, insane.

So, you felt berserk as you clawed at him and the blood streamed down his face?

BESIEGED

Synonym: Assaulted, attacked.

It seems as though you sometimes feel besieged by the requests of others, and tend to deny your own needs.

BETRAYED

Synonym: Deceived, fooled, duped, tricked, bamboozled, sucked in.

You once again allowed yourself to be vulnerable and are now left feeling betrayed.

BEWILDERED

Synonym: Confused, lost, troubled, misguided, baffled, astounded, befuddled.

You seem to feel bewildered that he sends flowers one week, then doesn't call for two weeks.

BEWITCHED

Synonym: Entranced, fascinated, enraptured, captivated.

It sounds like you were feeling bewitched at seeing a true pinball professional in action.

BIASED

Synonym: Prejudiced, swayed, influenced.

I'm sensing that you find it difficult to remain objective when you feel so biased about the situation.

BITCHY

Synonym: Malicious, arrogant, spiteful.

It sounds like you feel bitchy toward all men, and don't care who knows it.

BITTER

Synonym: Sarcastic, harsh, intense, acrimonious.

It seems like feeling bitter so long after the separation is only hurting you.

BIZARRE

Synonym: Odd, grotesque, unusual, fantastic, eccentric.

So, you feel really bizarre each time you wake from one of these fantastic dreams?

BLACKMAILED

Synonym: Extorted, bribed, coerced, forced.

She's threatening to tell your wife about the affair, and you're feeling blackmailed.

BLAMELESS

Synonym: Innocent, faultless, not guilty.

So, you feel blameless even though it was your idea, you drove the car, and then lied when they questioned you?

BLAMEWORTHY

Synonym: At fault, guilty, blamable.

I hear you saying you feel blameworthy but can't come up with any reason why he's abusing you.

BLASPHEMOUS

Synonym: Impious, profane, irreverent, irreligious.

He approached you sexually in church and you felt blasphemous.

BLEAK

Synonym: Desolate, disheartened, joyless, dreary, comfortless.

You felt bleak with winter rolling in and no one to be with for the holidays.

BLESSED

Synonym: Happy, glad, content, joyous.

Each time you consider the plight of the poor and homeless, you feel blessed and want to help?

BLINDED

Synonym: Misled, deceived, deluded.

So, you're telling me you felt blinded by his charm, even though you knew he was a con artist.

BLISSFUL

Synonym: Happy, delightful, joyful, ecstatic.

It sounds like you felt blissful when you learned the family would be staying at your home for the holidays.

BLOCKED

Synonym: Hindered, obstructed, checked, barred.

It sounds like you feel blocked in your career because of your unwillingness to play the business politics.

BLOWN AWAY

Synonym: Amazed, stunned.

Now you're feeling blown away that they've offered you the position, and regret getting so 'creative' when you wrote your resume.

BLOWN OFF

Synonym: Ignored, discounted.

I hear you felt blown off when you tried to speak, and then had to listen to someone else get credit for your idea.

BLOWN OVER

Synonym: Shocked, overwhelmed.

So, you felt blown over when you won the lottery, but now you're wondering where all the relatives came from?

BLUE

Synonym: Sad, melancholy,
                  depressed, moody.

Hearing that they might be taking the Smurfs off the air has left you feeling blue?

BLUNT

Synonym: Unfeeling, insensitive.

So, you felt blunt when you told her abortion was the only answer; now she's run off and you don't know what to do.

BOASTFUL

Synonym: Pretentious, egotistical, bragging.

It sounds like you felt boastful when you spoke of your achievements.

BLURRED

Synonym: Vague, unsure, indefinite.

You're feeling blurred by your love for her and can't believe she has a drug problem?

BOGGLED

Synonym: Bewildered, amazed, overwhelmed.

I'm hearing that you felt boggled when you realized the attraction was mutual.

BOISTEROUS

Synonym: Loud, obnoxious, noisy, rude, uproarious.

So, last night you felt boisterous at the party, and are now afraid you may have insulted the guests?

BOLD

Synonym: Brave, daring, fearless, intrepid.

You felt bold when you challenged him to a game, but your confidence dwindled when you began to lose.

BOORISH

Synonym: Rude, awkward, dull, clumsy, churlish.

It sounds like you felt boorish after you interrupted and corrected the child's story.

BORING

Synonym: Stupid, dull, tedious, monotonous.

Are you saying you felt boring at the party, but at the same time they all seemed superficial?

BOTTOMED OUT

Synonym: Low, depressed, hopeless.

What I think I'm hearing is that you feel bottomed out, and the time has come to seek treatment, is that right?

BRAINLESS

Synonym: Mindless, stupid, thoughtless.

You're feeling brainless because they assigned you such menial tasks?

BRAINWASHED

Synonym: Convinced, indoctrinated, conditioned.

It seems like you felt brainwashed by the time the salesman finished his pitch.

BRAVE

Synonym: Daring, confident, fearless, valiant, reckless, heroic.

It sounds like you were feeling brave when you decided to bungee jump, never considering you should have relieved yourself first ?

BRAZEN

Synonym: Rude, bold, forward, audacious.

I think you're saying you felt brazen by suggesting it's about time he took you out for dinner?

BREATHLESS

Synonym: Exhausted, choking, excited, panting.

It sounds like you felt breathless the very first time you hugged him.

BRILLIANT

Synonym: Ingenious, profound, dazzling, gleaming, intelligent, penetrating.

The professor's question had everyone stumped, but you felt brilliant when you answered it correctly?

BRISK

Synonym: Active, lively, energetic, sharp, invigorated.

It sounds like walking the ocean shoreline at sunrise left you feeling brisk and refreshed.

BROKEN

Synonym: Shattered, smashed, destroyed, crushed, injured, ruined.

The unexpected death of your father seems to have left you feeling broken.

BROKENHEARTED

Synonym: Despondent, hurt, crushed, sad, grieved.

I'm hearing you say you feel brokenhearted that the relationship ended, even though it seemed inevitable?

BRUISED

Synonym: Wounded, beaten, hurt, injured, damaged.

I sense that you felt bruised when your mother made a comment about your weight.

BRUSHED OFF

Synonym: Rejected, dismissed, discarded, repelled, abolished, expelled.

You tried to enter into the conversation, but felt brushed off when they ignored you?

BRUTALIZED

Synonym: Abused, tormented, tortured.

It sounds like you feel brutalized the moment her tirade begins.

BRUTISH

Synonym: Savage, beastly, degenerate.

It made you feel brutish when your dad said to just drown the kittens and be done with it.

BUBBLY

Synonym: Happy, giggly, effervescent.

You immediately felt bubbly the minute he suggested you jump in the hot tub together?

BULLIED

Synonym: Harassed, threatened, teased, domineered.

I'm hearing that you felt bullied when the new policies at work seemed to only apply to you.

BUOYANT

Synonym: Light, spirited, jovial, cheerful, happy.

You felt buoyant when they agreed to finance the boat and now you're sinking in debt?

BURDENED

Synonym: Overwhelmed, obligated, overloaded, encumbered.

I hear you saying you feel burdened with your aging parents just when your own life presents so many opportunities.

BURNED OUT

Synonym: Exhausted, debilitated, worn, weak, devitalized.

I think you're saying that when you feel burned out at work and at home, you need a few days away to regroup.

BUSHED

Synonym: Tired, exhausted.

Are you saying you feel bushed after eight hours of gardening?

BUTCHERED

Synonym: Botched, slaughtered, mutilated, destroyed.

So, you felt butchered when she cut you up with her crude remarks; she had been so sweet until then?

BYPASSED

Synonym: Overlooked, ignored, left out.

t sounds like you felt bypassed when the boss implemented a new program in your department without asking for your input.

CALLOUS

Synonym: Hard, insensitive, heartless, cruel, unfeeling, cold, unresponsive.

hear you saying that you're feeling callous about love to avoid pain, but that attitude also is keeping you from experiencing joy.

CALM

Synonym: Placid, serene, tranquil, peaceful, gentle, relaxed.

Sitting by the waterfall in the mountains was the last time you really felt calm?

CAPABLE

Synonym: Competent, proficient, able, intelligent.

So you feel capable about the new position and it's more money, but t just doesn't interest you.

CAPRICIOUS

Synonym: Impulsive, unpredictable, whimsical, fickle.

It sounds like you felt capricious when you got up and danced in the spotlight to "Saturday Night Fever".

CAREFUL

Synonym: Cautious, deliberate, prudent, meticulous, vigilant.

I hear you were feeling careful when you laid the baby on the bed, and were shocked to find her on the floor crying.

CARELESS

Synonym: Remiss, reckless, indifferent, rash, negligent.

You're feeling careless that you might have been responsible for the fire with your cigarette butt.

CATALYZED

Synonym: Inspired, stimulated, encouraged, invigorated, caused.

I hear you felt catalyzed by her stimulating ideas when she was around, but now she's gone.

CAUTIOUS

Synonym: Careful, watchful,
                wary, circumspect.

You seem to be feeling cautious
regarding life-altering decisions
right now.

CEREBRAL

Synonym: Intellectual, inventive,
                creative.

So, you felt quite cerebral as you attempted to explain the meaning
of life to the group, but saw nothing but dull, blank faces staring back
at you.

CERTAIN

Synonym: Positive, confident, assured, convinced.

You feel certain of your abilities on the job until the rumors start
again.

CHALLENGED

Synonym: Threatened, denounced, defiled, doubted.

He said girls can't beat boys at anything important and that made
you feel challenged?

CHARITABLE

Synonym: Beneficent, generous, kind, philanthropic, benevolent.

It sounds like you felt charitable when you donated to the shelter, but then found out they bought a color TV for the staff.

CHARMING

Synonym: Enchanting, irresistible, charismatic, fascinating, intriguing, tantalizing, titillating.

I'm sensing that you felt charming after four hours of good conversation, then he stuffed you in a cab and sent you home.

CHEAP

Synonym: Tight, thrifty, stingy.

So, you started to feel cheap when the staff took up an office collection to buy you a new tie.

CHEATED

Synonym: Victimized, swindled, tricked, deceived, scammed, foiled.

You began feeling cheated when you realized the rare coin you bought was dated 35 B.C.?

CHEERFUL

Synonym: Happy, gay, joyful, merry, pleasant, sparkling.

You felt cheerful when he broke up with her; does that seem right?

CHILDLIKE

Synonym: Innocent, ingenuous, spontaneous, natural.

It sounds like you felt childlike flying a kite at your age.

CHIVALROUS

Synonym: Valiant, noble, courteous, brave, gallant.

It sounds like you felt chivalrous when you changed a flat tire for the elderly couple.

CHOKED UP

Synonym: Overcome, emotional.

So, you usually feel choked up when the National Anthem is played?

CIVIL

Synonym: Polite, refined, courteous, formal.

So, you're telling me you were able to feel civil toward her ex-husband, even though he was rude and demeaning?

CLASSY

Synonym: Stylish, elegant, tasteful, dignified.

It sounds like you felt classy when you got a limo ride to the theater until he asked you to chip in for gas.

CLEVER

Synonym: Adroit, ingenious, skillful, expert, shrewd.

You felt clever with your sarcastic remarks, but now it seems like it cost you a lot of friends.

CLOSE

Synonym: Intimate, familiar, confidential.

Even though you'd only just met, you felt close almost immediately.

CLUMSY

Synonym: Awkward, unwieldy, gawkish, inept.

I sense that you felt clumsy after you fell down the stairs in front of everyone.

COARSE

Synonym: Crude, vulgar, obscene.

I sense you were feeling coarse when the kids heard you swearing in the garage, and now they're using the same language?

COCKY

Synonym: Over-confident, jaunty, reckless, impudent.

So, you felt cocky quitting your job to get into poultry farming, but now the profits seem like chicken feed.

COERCED

Synonym: Impelled, compelled, forced, threatened.

So, you're saying that you felt coerced into signing the health spa agreement by the pushy salesman?

COGNIZANT

Synonym: Aware, conscious, perceptive, observant.

It sounds like you feel cognizant of the fact that your co-dependent behavior only perpetuates the family problems.

COLD

Synonym: Unfeeling, frigid, indifferent, apathetic.

I'm sensing that the superficial atmosphere at the singles' bars leaves you feeling cold.

COMBATIVE

Synonym: Aggressive, warlike, competitive.

It sounds like the child's resistance to following the rules has you feeling combative, and you're fearing you could become abusive?

COMFORTABLE

Synonym: Contented, satisfied, relaxed, untroubled, cheerful, happy.

I hear you saying that you feel comfortable just snuggling with her at the end of a long, hard week.

COMMENDABLE

Synonym: Praiseworthy, excellent, laudable.

It sounds like your daughter felt commendable when she brought home another great report card, but you couldn't interrupt your soap operas.

COMMITTED

Synonym: Dedicated, obligated, empowered.

In spite of all the politics involved, you still feel committed to the work of the organization?

COMPATIBLE

Synonym: Cooperative, agreeable, harmonious, congruous.

It seems like a long time since you've felt compatible with a member of the opposite sex.

COMPELLED

Synonym: Forced, driven, obsessed, coerced.

It sounds like you're feeling compelled to work even when you don't feel like it because you can't allow your kids to suffer.

COMPETENT

Synonym: Able, capable, qualified, skilled, satisfactory.

I'm hearing that you feel competent enough to raise your child alone, but now you have to convince the court.

COMPETITIVE

Synonym: Rival, antagonistic, opposing, battling.

It sounds like you were feeling quite competitive when you challenged your friend to a game of pool, but now you need an optometrist referral.

COMPLACENT

Synonym: Satisfied, contented, passive, smug.

You're feeling complacent about your work even though you know you could do much better.

COMPLIANT

Synonym: Obedient, agreeable, docile, yielding.

So, you felt compliant with the rules, even though they seemed stupid to you?

COMPOSED

Synonym: Confident, poised, relaxed, untroubled, sensible, calm.

It sounds like you felt composed throughout the proceedings despite the awful things being said about you.

COMPROMISED

Synonym: Jeopardized, endangered, imperiled, betrayed.

You settled for less than your price for the house, and now you're feeling compromised?

COMPULSIVE

Synonym: Passionate, enthusiastic, obsessive.

It sounds like you feel compulsive about washing your hands even when you know they're clean.

CONCEITED

Synonym: Arrogant, egotistic, vain, narcissistic.

So, you're not sure if you feel conceited, or are really perfect in every way?

CONCERNED

Synonym: Worried, caring, involved, bothered.

I hear how concerned you felt when your daughter came in after curfew.

CONDEMNED

Synonym: Denounced, censured, judged, guilty, convicted, damned.

It sounds like you felt condemned by their accusations, even though they were unfounded.

CONFIDENT

Synonym: Certain, positive,
           sure, able, fearless, bold.

It seems like you feel confident in your ability to do public speaking; all you have to do is brush up on the subject?

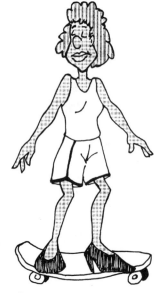

CONFLICTED

Synonym: Torn, disputed, struggling, contrary.

This decision affects a number of people differently and you're feeling conflicted?

CONFOUNDED

Synonym: Perplexed, confused,
           puzzled, doubtful.

You seem to feel confounded that your lottery numbers have not been drawn after all these weeks.

CONFRONTATIONAL

Synonym: Argumentative, quarrelsome, controversial.

It sounds like you felt confrontational when you questioned the new policies at the staff meeting.

CONFUSED

Synonym: Confounded, puzzled, bewildered, troubled, unsettled, bothered.

So, you feel confused by all you hear about damage to the environment, and wonder what kind of planet we're leaving our grandchildren.

CONGENIAL

Synonym: Friendly, agreeable, compatible, suitable, harmonious, pleasant.

I'm hearing that you felt congenial at the conference even though you didn't know anyone.

CONNECTED

Synonym: Related, belonging, coupled, associated, relevant, united.

It seems that after spending four days with the disaster survivors, you felt very connected to them and your team of counselors?

CONSIDERATE

Synonym: Kind, thoughtful, polite, charitable.

You say that you feel considerate by sending cards for no real reason, but is it fair to expect others to do the same?

CONSPICUOUS

Synonym: Glaring, outstanding, famed, notorious, prominent.

The chemotherapy is causing your hair to fall out and you feel conspicuous, yet it may be saving your life.

CONSTRAINED

Synonym: Stifled, forced, compelled, coerced, pressured.

It sounds like you feel constrained by etiquette, and can't really be yourself at these formal dinner parties your wife expects you to attend.

CONSTRUCTIVE

Synonym: Valuable, helpful, useful, creative, effective, productive.

I hear you felt constructive when you helped the kids with their homework, but learned many of your answers were wrong?

CONTAMINATED

Synonym: Dirty, polluted, corrupt, defiled, infected.

So, you felt contaminated the moment you entered the subway system, and you still have two more weeks left in the city?

CONTENTED

Synonym: Satisfied, agreeable, pleased, happy.

It sounds like you feel contented just spending time with those you love.

CONTEMPTUOUS

Synonym: Disrespectful, scornful, nasty.

So, his harassment left you feeling contemptuous, and all you can think of is getting even.

CONTEMPTIBLE

Synonym: Mean, nasty, degenerate, hateful, worthless.

Now you feel contemptible every time you think about how you exploited your friends; what can you do about it?

CONTRARY

Synonym: Opposed, contrasted, argumentative.

You find yourself feeling contrary every time she opens her mouth, just because you find her so irritating?

CONTRITE

Synonym: Sorry, humbled, repentant, regretful.

Once you realized you had hurt your friend's feelings, you felt contrite.

CONTROVERSIAL

Synonym: Questionable, argumentative, doubtful, debatable, suspect.

It sounds like you felt controversial when you tried to defend your position at the party, but you still stand by your beliefs.

CONVICTED

Synonym: Condemned, guilty, sentenced, doomed, judged.

It seems that their comments left you feeling convicted before you even got to tell your side of the story.

CONVINCED

Synonym: Certain, assured, converted, changed, persuaded.

You say you feel convinced that things will work out eventually, but what steps are you taking now?

COOL

Synonym: Calm, restrained, unruffled, composed, indifferent.

So, you felt cool having the only air conditioner in the projects, but last night it was swiped?

COOPERATIVE

Synonym: Helpful, agreeable, useful, sociable, concurring.

So, you really like feeling cooperative, and wish everyone did.

CORRUPTED

Synonym: Perverted, wicked, depraved, defiled, adulterated.

You feel corrupted; he made you do things you never thought you would.

COURAGEOUS

Synonym: Brave, gallant, daring, bold, fearless.

I'm hearing that you felt courageous enough to offer help at the accident scene in spite of your fears.

COURTEOUS

Synonym: Polite, civil, friendly, cordial, respectful, reverent.

When the preachers first came to the door you felt courteous, but they wouldn't let up until you chased them off your property?

COVETOUS

Synonym: Greedy, selfish, envious, desirous.

It sounds like you felt covetous when you saw your co-worker's new summer home.

COWARDLY

Synonym: Timid, shy, fearful, scared, panicky, chicken, afraid.

It makes you feel cowardly to move from the old neighborhood, but you just don't feel safe anymore.

CRABBY

Synonym: Irritable, grouchy, cranky, offensive.

You feel crabby after an hour in rush hour traffic, and can't respond to the kids mobbing you when you drive up?

CRAMPED

Synonym: Restricted, confined, uncomfortable, restrained.

You're saying you feel cramped in the dorm, but your dad says you're stuck there until you bring your grades up?

CRASS

Synonym: Vulgar, ignorant, gross, stupid.

The ethnic joke offended your neighbor and left you feeling crass?

CRAZY

Synonym: Insane, mad, loony, demented.

It sounds like you felt crazy when the psychotic client's story made perfect sense to you.

CREATIVE

Synonym: Artistic, inventive, original, productive.

You seem to be saying that you feel most creative when you have time to yourself.

CREDIBLE

Synonym: Truthful, likely, honest, reliable, trustworthy.

I'm hearing that you felt credible when you were able to give statistics to back up your facts.

CREEPY

Synonym: Sneaky, cowering, groveling.

He gives you a creepy feeling every time he comes in, but you're not sure why.

CRIMPED

Synonym: Cramped, confined, restrained.

It sounds like you felt crimped when she told you that you were overstepping your authority?

CRIPPLED

Synonym: Disabled, deformed, maimed, damaged, impaired, broken.

You're telling me that you feel crippled by thoughts of emotional intimacy?

CRITICAL

Synonym: Observant, demanding, disapproving, sarcastic, sharp, biting.

I hear that you felt critical when you told your cousin she talks too much.

CRITICIZED

Synonym: Censured, studied, examined, nitpicked, condemned.

It sounds like you feel criticized every time someone offers feedback.

CROSS

Synonym: Angry, irritable, annoyed, jumpy.

It sounds like you felt cross when the neighbor's dogs woke you, and you were unable to go back to sleep?

CROSSED

Synonym: Betrayed, exposed, interrogated.

So, you felt crossed when you found that your friend had broken your confidence?

CROWDED

Synonym: Squeezed, crushed, pressured.

I'm hearing that you are feeling crowded by the demands of others.

CRUCIFIED

Synonym: Tormented, tortured, executed, destroyed.

I hear that you felt crucified when they fired you for drinking on the job, but let the others off with a warning.

CRUDE

Synonym: Coarse, harsh, rude, rough, unpolished.

She overheard your remark about her weight and now you're feeling crude?

CRUEL

Synonym: Wicked, evil, sinful, depraved, spiteful, degenerate, gross, outrageous.

It sounds like you felt cruel when you joined in the office gossip, until you resolved never to do it again.

CRUMMY

Synonym: Cheap, worthless, miserable, filthy.

You're saying he always makes you feel crummy because he's humiliated you ever since you were kids?

CUCKOO

Synonym: Silly, stupid, weird, insane.

So, you felt cuckoo when you told the group your favorite thing to do is bird watching, but feel entitled to your own interests?

CUDDLESOME

Synonym: Affectionate, warm, snugly.

Often you feel cuddlesome and don't want sex, but he gets really confused by that?

CULPABLE

Synonym: Guilty, punishable, blamable, blameworthy.

The phony lawsuit was won based on your testimony and you feel culpable?

CUMBERSOME

Synonym: Uncomfortable, clumsy, awkward.

I hear you feel really cumbersome on the dance floor, but can't think of any other way to meet people?

CUNNING

Synonym: Shrewd, sly, crafty, deceptive.

So, you felt cunning as you planned your revenge, but are glad that you had the good sense not to follow through.

CURIOUS

Synonym: Inquisitive, inquiring, analytical, nosey, meddling, prying.

So, you're saying you watched the talk show because you were feeling curious about lesbians and found yourself strangely attracted.

CURSED

Synonym: Damned, hopeless, doomed, afflicted, possessed.

You feel cursed, as if good things only happen to other people?

CURTAILED

Synonym: Cramped, stopped, halted, diminished.

It sounds like you feel curtailed in program development by the appalling lack of funds.

CYNICAL

Synonym: Sarcastic, unbelieving, sneering, sardonic.

It sounds like watching the news leaves you feeling cynical about the future, and you don't know if life is worth living.

DAFFY

Synonym: Silly, stupid, foolish, crazy, asinine, ridiculous.

So, it makes you feel daffy to admit you really enjoy Saturday morning cartoons?

DAMAGED

Synonym: Bruised, wounded, hurt, wasted, deprived.

The scars from the surgery make you feel damaged, and you don't want him looking at you?

DAMNED

Synonym: Cursed, doomed, condemned, convicted, worthless.

You feel damned by what you've done, and say God could never forgive you.

DAZED

Synonym: Bewildered, confused, baffled, perplexed, doubtful.

You laid there feeling dazed after being hit by a car you never saw coming.

DAZZLED

Synonym: Surprised, astonished, amazed, impressed, stunned.

So, you felt dazzled by the depth, humor, and intelligence of the shy, quiet man in the corner of the room.

DEADENED

Synonym: Paralyzed, impaired, repressed, incapacitated, exhausted.

It sounds like you felt deadened by the news that your child needed major surgery.

DEBAUCHED

Synonym: Depraved, wicked, defiled, corrupted, debased.

I'm hearing that you felt debauched by the construction workers' crude remarks as you passed by.

DEBILITATED

Synonym: Weakened, incapacitated, injured, inactivated, crippled.

The combination of acute depression and P.M.S. has left you feeling debilitated?

DECEIVED

Synonym: Fooled, duped, betrayed, conned, tricked, cheated.

So, you felt deceived when you donated and then discovered that the Deceased Widows of War Veterans was not a legitimate charity?

DECEPTIVE

Synonym: Dishonest, tricky, unreliable, lying, misleading.

You didn't report all your tips on your 1040 from and now you're feeling deceptive.

DECISIVE

Synonym: Determined, conclusive, certain, definitive, final.

You seem to feel decisive in your plan to move.

DECREPIT

Synonym: Weak, frail, old, senile.

You sound surprised that two hours on the basketball court with the kids would leave you feeling decrepit.

DEDICATED

Synonym: Devoted, determined, faithful, loyal.

You seem to feel dedicated to helping the homeless in spite of the red tape.

DEFENSIVE

Synonym: Protective, watchful, shielding, careful.

I notice you feel very defensive when someone mentions how abusive your husband is to you.

DEFICIENT

Synonym: Inadequate, meager, failing, incompetent, impotent.

It's only when the other kids ridicule you that you feel deficient?

DEFILED

Synonym: Violated, adulterated, corrupted, polluted, debased.

I think I hear you saying that you felt defiled when the drunken stranger kept grabbing at you.

DEFINITE

Synonym: Sure, positive, specific, certain, determined, exact.

I'm sensing that you feel definite in your plan to leave and start a new life.

DEFLATED

Synonym: Empty, defeated, exhausted, whipped.

When you realized you couldn't afford the new tires, you felt deflated?

DEFRAUDED

Synonym: Cheated, betrayed, tricked, deceived, duped.

It sounds like you felt defrauded when the knives you ordered from a TV ad melted in the dishwasher.

DEFUNCT

Synonym: Dead, lifeless, extinct, devoid, mortified.

I think you're saying you felt defunct after attempting Richard Simmons' "Sweatin to the Oldies" workout.

DEFUSED

Synonym: Calm, sedated, harmless, powerless, gentle.

After a session with a crisis counselor, you felt defused and relieved.

DEGRADED

Synonym: Humbled, disgraced, depraved, diminished, deteriorated.

It sounds like you felt degraded after the rape, which is precisely how the attacker wanted you to feel.

DEHUMANIZED

Synonym: Humiliated, shamed, disgraced, embarrassed, humbled.

As you waited in the unemployment line, you began feeling dehumanized?

DEJECTED

Synonym: Sad, depressed, grieved, sorrowful, dispirited.

You say you felt dejected when the promotion was given to one with less seniority.

DELIGHTED

Synonym: Happy, excited, pleased, gratified, enchanted, jubilant.

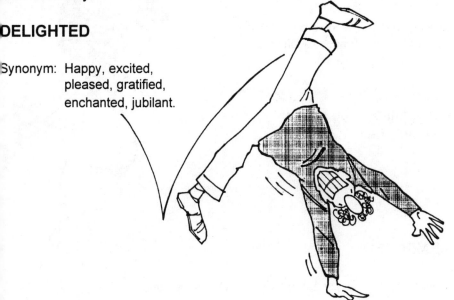

I'm hearing that you were delighted to find that you have so much in common with her.

DELINQUENT

Synonym: Negligent, faulty, derelict, remiss, careless.

So, you're feeling delinquent for not paying child support.

DELIRIOUS

Synonym: Mad, insane, demented, hallucinating, crazy, irrational.

The eleven hour intervention with the family left you feeling delirious, but you're sure you helped them.

DELUDED

Synonym: Deceived, fooled, betrayed, tricked.

I think you're saying you felt deluded after Nixon was exposed.

DEMANDING

Synonym: Difficult, critical, hard, fussy, troublesome, exacting.

It seems as though you feel demanding if you ask for anyone's help.

DEMENTED

Synonym: Crazy, unbalanced, mad, insane, delirious.

After listening to him twist the truth so many times, you started feeling demented yourself?

DEMOLISHED

Synonym: Ruined, trashed, destroyed, devastated, obliterated.

When they scrapped the plans for your project and cut it from the budget, you felt demolished?

DEMORALIZED

Synonym: Sad, weakened, depressed, hopeless, depraved, unnerved.

It sounds like the staff felt demoralized when they weren't appreciated or rewarded.

DEPENDENT

Synonym: Subordinate, needful, weak, helpless, indigent.

I think you are saying you can't leave this abusive man because you feel dependent emotionally and financially.

DEPLETED

Synonym: Spent, wasted, consumed, exhausted, drained, used up.

It seems you feel depleted after a 60-hour week and you need to be pampered.

DEPRAVED

Synonym: Evil, corrupted, bad, crooked, perverted.

You let him talk you into going to see the X-rated movie, but felt depraved afterward?

DEPRECIATED

Synonym: Slandered, slurred, disgraced, slighted, censured.

It sounds like you felt depreciated when your wife said you don't do enough around the house.

DEPRESSED

Synonym: Sad, discouraged, hopeless, pessimistic, disheartened, disparaged.

It seems that you're depressed by the lack of close relationships in your life.

DEPRIVED

Synonym: Cheated, left out, stripped.

It sounds like you felt deprived when your brother inherited every-thing except the mean bulldog.

DESECRATED

Synonym: Fouled, adulterated, spoiled.

I hear that you felt desecrated after the one-night stand with a stranger.

DESERTED

Synonym: Forsaken, abandoned, relinquished, neglected, shunned.

Your best friend has moved out of town and now you feel deserted?

DESERVING

Synonym: Worthy, entitled, fitting, appropriate.

It seems you felt deserving of a standing ovation after your performance.

DESIRABLE

Synonym: Seductive, charming, alluring, fascinating.

I hear that you felt desirable when they gave you all that attention.

DESIROUS

Synonym: Lustful, enthusiastic, wanting, needing, willing.

I hear that you are feeling desirous of a long-term relationship, yet you are feeling ambivalent as well.

DESOLATE

Synonym: Abandoned, isolated, forsaken, alone, downcast.

When you called the crisis center, you were feeling desolate, but now you're finding some hope?

DESPAIRING

Synonym: Miserable, sad, hopeless, helpless, despondent.

I'm sensing that you feel despairing enough to consider suicide.

DESPERATE

Synonym: Wild, careless, rash, drastic, trapped.

It sounds like you robbed the bank because you were feeling desperate for money.

DESPICABLE

Synonym: Base, crude, mean, contemptible, reprehensible.

It sounds like you felt despicable when you cheated during the playoffs.

DESPISED

Synonym: Hated, condemned, scorned, loathed, cursed.

I'm hearing you felt despised when your child told you he never wanted to see you again.

DESPONDENT

Synonym: Discouraged, hopeless, depressed, dejected.

So, you felt despondent when no one seemed to care about your problems.

DESTINED

Synonym: Inevitable, doomed, fated, looming, imminent.

You seem to feel destined to repeat unhealthy behavior patterns in spite of the fact that you can change them.

DETACHED

Synonym: Separated, apathetic, withdrawn, disengaged, uninvolved.

You've seen so much poverty in your work that you now feel detached and need a career change?

DETERMINED

Synonym: Decided, resolved, agreed, stubborn, strong-minded, resolute.

You've set some ambitious goals for yourself, but feel determined you can meet them.

DEVASTATED

Synonym: Destroyed, ruined, ravaged, wasted.

Your best friend has run off with your husband and you feel devastated.

DEVILISH

Synonym: Wicked, evil, fiendish, inhuman.

So you say you felt devilish when you put the whoopee cushion on the teacher's chair.

DEVIOUS

Synonym: Sly, dishonest, insidious, crafty, shrewd, foxy.

It sounds like you felt devious getting him to the alcohol intervention session under false pretenses.

DEVOTED

Synonym: Faithful, dutiful, constant, loyal, dedicated, believing.

I hear you're feeling devoted to keeping your family together in spite of the many problems.

DIABOLIC

Synonym: Evil, wicked, fiendish, devilish, impious.

Planning your mother-in-law's demise made you feel diabolic; what about the consequences?

DICTATORIAL

Synonym: Arrogant, egotistic, authoritarian, pompous, autocratic.

So, you're saying that you feel dictatorial when you have to remind your teenager to do her chores?

DIFFIDENT

Synonym: Restrained, shy, bashful, humble, timid.

It sounds as though you feel diffident whenever you are around people you don't know well.

DIGNIFIED

Synonym: Majestic, cultured, refined, distinguished, imposing, elegant.

You like feeling dignified but don't want to be pretentious?

DILIGENT

Synonym: Hard working, industrious, persistent, careful, earnest.

You always feel diligent about your research efforts, but deadlines take all the enjoyment out of it.

DIMINISHED

Synonym: Lessened, reduced, depreciated, discredited, denounced.

It seems like you felt diminished by their remarks about your qualifications.

DIPLOMATIC

Synonym: Gracious, shrewd, tactful, polite, astute, artful.

It sounds like you felt diplomatic when you stepped in to help settle the dispute, but now they're both mad at you.

DISAFFECTED

Synonym: Indifferent, estranged, alienated, unfriendly, repelled.

All the pleas for donations at Christmas leave you feeling disaffected, but they still spoil the spirit of the season?

DISAPPOINTED

Synonym: Dissatisfied, discouraged, depressed, disconcerted.

Is it correct to assume you were disappointed when no one showed up for the game?

DISARMED

Synonym: Convinced, persuaded, impelled, moved, seduced.

You seem to feel disarmed by the psychic's insight regarding your desire for wealth, fame and love.

DISCARDED

Synonym: Thrown away, rejected, junked, worn out, useless, obsolete.

Waking up in the dumpster with a hangover made you feel discarded; do you remember how you got there?

DISCONNECTED

Synonym: Incoherent, incongruous, disjointed, separated.

Sometimes you feel disconnected from everything around you; do you ever hear voices?

DISCONSOLATE

Synonym: Dismal, dejected, sad, melancholy, hopeless, gloomy.

I hear you saying that you feel disconsolate over the breakup of this marriage.

DISCONTENTED

Synonym: Sad, malcontented, unhappy, disgruntled.

You seem to be feeling discontented with your present state of life.

DISCOURAGED

Synonym: Dismal, downcast, melancholy, depressed, restricted, sad.

These recent financial setbacks have left you feeling discouraged?

DISCOURTEOUS

Synonym: Impolite, vulgar, rude, impudent, crude.

Kicking people out of your express line makes you feel discourteous, but rules are rules.

DISCREDITED

Synonym: Reproached, censured, criticized, blamed, condemned.

It sounds like you felt discredited when the newspaper printed an entirely different version of your story.

DISCREET

Synonym: Prudent, decent, polite, considerate, thoughtful, judicious.

When you described the harassment to your supervisor you were feeling discreet, but things are getting out of hand?

DISGRACED

Synonym: Humiliated, slandered, ridiculed, shamed, dishonest.

Having to tell anyone that you've been married three times before makes you feel disgraced?

DISGUSTED

Synonym: Offended, revolted, insulted, outraged, sickened, shocked.

So, you're feeling disgusted with the rivalrous sensationalism of current talk show topics.

DISHEARTENED

Synonym: Dismayed, depressed, humiliated, discouraged.

It sounds like you felt disheartened when your wife told you there is another man in her life.

DISHONEST

Synonym: Sneaky, tricky, deceptive, shady, corrupt, cunning.

I hear that you felt dishonest when you told the woman you've never been married before.

DISHONORABLE

Synonym: Offensive, shameful, disgraced, ignoble, infamous.

Being asked to leave the dojo has you feeling dishonorable, but you've obviously done nothing wrong.

DISILLUSIONED

Synonym: Disappointed, disenchanted, defeated, beaten.

It seems as though your experiences have left you feeling disillusioned about love.

DISINTERESTED

Synonym: Indifferent, unconcerned, impartial.

It sounds like until you met this special person, you felt totally disinterested in new relationships.

DISLIKED

Synonym: Deplored, detested, condemned, hated.

It seems as though you felt disliked when they relegated you to another table at the banquet.

DISLOYAL

Synonym: Unfaithful, false, dishonest, traitorous, perfidious.

It sounds like you felt disloyal when you cheated on your husband.

DISMAL

Synonym: Gloomy, cold, dark, miserable, depressed, sorrowful, horrid.

Once all the leaves have fallen from the trees, you start feeling dismal, and only springtime can bring you out of it?

DISMAYED

Synonym: Anxious, fearful, dreaded.

He misunderstood when you told him you needed some space, and now you feel dismayed that he may be gone.

DISOBEDIENT

Synonym: Defiant, rebellious, unruly, insubordinate.

Your parents warned you to stay away from the party, but you felt disobedient and went anyway?

DISORGANIZED

Synonym: Confused, scattered, deranged, jumbled, scrambled, confounded.

You can't be trusted to take your medication because you're feeling too disorganized right now?

DISPASSIONATE

Synonym: Fair, just, impartial, judicial.

You say it's difficult to feel dispassionate when you have confronted a child abuser.

DISPENSABLE

Synonym: Useless, unneeded, excessive, trivial, unnecessary, removable.

So, you felt dispensable when you discovered they'd given the assignment to someone else.

DISSATISFIED

Synonym: Displeased, unhappy, unsatisfied, discontented, ungratified.

I sense that you are feeling dissatisfied with your current living arrangements, yet are afraid of change.

DISSUADED

Synonym: Discouraged, deterred, prevented, hindered, thwarted, impeded.

I hear you felt dissuaded from joining the circus when you remembered you detest clowns.

DISTRACTED

Synonym: Troubled, confused, bewildered, frenzied, puzzled, perplexed.

It sounds like you felt distracted from your work when you recalled the events of last night.

DISTRAUGHT

Synonym: Troubled, worried, bothered, harassed, confused.

I hear that you felt distraught when you realized your paycheck wouldn't cover the bills.

DISTRESSED

Synonym: Anguished, miserable, anxious, worried, perplexed, wretched.

When you learned your mother was in the emergency room, you felt distressed and didn't know where to turn?

DISTRUSTFUL

Synonym: Suspicious, doubting, disbelieving, cautious.

I hear you saying you feel distrustful of men in general because of your negative experiences in the past.

DISTURBED

Synonym: Upset, troubled, annoyed, agitated, disordered, aggravated.

You want to believe the story she told you, but parts of it leave you feeling disturbed?

DIVINE

Synonym: Heavenly, spiritual,
Godlike, omnipotent,
supernatural, perfect.

Each week you faithfully watch
the evangelist and his message
makes you feel divine?

DOCILE

Synonym: Humble, meek, mild,
submissive, obedient,
gentle, accommodating.

All day long you plan what you're going to say, but as soon as he
walks in you feel docile and the issues never get resolved?

DOMINEERING

Synonym: Oppressive, bullying, autocratic, tyrannical, despotic.

It seems you felt domineering when you forced the child to come to
church despite her protests.

DOOMED

Synonym: Destroyed, ruined, cursed, convicted, ill-fated, condemned.

It sounds like you felt
doomed when the
governor stopped the
General Assistance
program.

DOUBTFUL

Synonym: Uncertain, wavering, suspicious, unsure, questioning.

I hear you saying you're feeling doubtful that your son can maintain a monogamous relationship.

DRAINED

Synonym: Sapped, weakened, dissipated, exhausted, empty, wasted.

When he told you he lost another job, you just felt drained; it's hard to feel anger anymore.

DREAMY

Synonym: Unreal, impractical, fanciful, whimsical, illusory, romantic.

It seems that you feel dreamy as you lie on the beach and watch clouds roll by.

DRIVEN

Synonym: Obsessed, forced, impelled, directed.

You have plenty of money, but you just feel driven to accumulate more even though you know it's killing you?

DUBIOUS

Synonym: Doubtful, perplexed, unclear, obscure, indecisive, hesitant.

I hear that you feel dubious about ordering the beauty cream that Ernest Borgnine promotes.

DUMB

Synonym: Stupid, feeble-minded, impaired, foolish, moronic.

It sounds like you felt dumb when you joined the Hair Club for Men, and then discovered it was for BALD men.

DUMBFOUNDED

Synonym: Surprised, astonished, amazed, puzzled.

So, you felt dumbfounded to learn that almost everyone gets a letter like that from Ed McMahon?

DUTIFUL

Synonym: Obedient, faithful, devoted, dedicated, respectful, conscientious.

It sounds like you felt dutiful when you turned your parents in for marijuana possession.

EAGER

Synonym: Anxious, enthusiastic, excited, sincere, fervent, willing.

What you're saying is, you were feeling eager to explain but he wouldn't take your call?

EARNEST

Synonym: Sincere, warm, honest, ardent, determined, persistent, dedicated.

So, you felt earnest when you proposed the deal but he called you a crook?

EASY

Synonym: Comfortable, calm, peaceful, secure, relaxed, restful.

You feel really easy around her even though you're normally quite shy?

EBULLIENT

Synonym: Bubbly, excited, effervescent, vivacious, exhilarated.

So, you were already feeling ebullient when the second bottle of champagne was opened.

ECSTATIC

Synonym: Happy, delighted, overjoyed, rapturous.

What I hear you saying is that you were feeling so ecstatic that the deal went through that you didn't read the fine print?

EDGY

Synonym: Irritable, quick-tempered, excitable, impatient, touchy.

Sounds like you feel edgy every time your neighbor practices his guitar.

EERIE

Synonym: Weird, strange, frightful, superstitious, fearful.

The creaking floorboards in the attic made you feel eerie?

EFFEMINATE

Synonym: Unmanly, feminine, womanly, ladylike, matronly, maidenly.

The underwear she bought you makes you feel effeminate, but she says she really likes it.

EGOTISTIC

Synonym: Self-centered, boastful,
arrogant, insolent,
snobbish, aloof, cocky.

Sounds like you felt egotistic because no one had a car like yours, but now it's no fun driving around alone?

ELATED

Synonym: Excited, inspired, aroused, delighted, enthusiastic, encouraged.

I hear that you're feeling elated that your daughter made the principal's list again?

ELECTRIFIED

Synonym: Energized, powered, driven, excited, charged.

You feel electrified by thunderstorms?

ELEGANT

Synonym: Dignified, beautiful, well-bred, tasteful, fashionable, classy.

You felt elegant as you skipped out the door in your new dress, and then fell off the porch into the bushes?

ELEVATED

Synonym: Heightened, raised, praised, dignified, eminent, noble.

I hear you saying you felt elevated when you moved into her penthouse?

ELIMINATED

Synonym: Blackballed, ostracized, banished, dumped, ditched, marooned.

I hear you saying you felt eliminated when they didn't cast you in the laxative commercial.

ELOQUENT

Synonym: Articulate, fluent, outspoken, persuasive, copious, talkative.

It sounds like you felt eloquent delivering your speech, and then found out you were mistakenly in the Mensa conference room?

EMANCIPATED

Synonym: Liberated, set-free, released, freed, unburdened, delivered.

So you felt emancipated after you quit your job, but now you're not so sure?

EMPATHIC

Synonym: Understanding, pitying, compassionate, sympathetic, benevolent.

So you were feeling empathic toward the child molester, at the same time hating the things he did.

EMPHATIC

Synonym: Assured, important, confident, positive, energetic, strong, forceful.

It sounds like you're feeling emphatic about trying to contact Dr. Kevorkian?

EMPTY

Synonym: Unfulfilled, hollow, barren, wanting, void, abandoned.

I hear you saying you feel empty by the thought of never having any children.

ENAMORED

Synonym: Fascinated, enchanted, enraptured, delighted, overwhelmed.

You felt so enamored by the mountains of Montana that you're packing it in and going there?

ENCOURAGED

Synonym: Inspired, enthusiastic, supported, helped, confident, fearless.

Now that we've talked you feel encouraged; that always makes it worthwhile.

ENDANGERED

Synonym: Imperiled, exposed, jeopardized, fraught.

I hear you feel endangered by the crack house across the street?

ENDEARED

Synonym: Valued, treasured, loved, prized, cherished.

It sounds like you felt endeared by his sweetly seductive talk, and then never heard from him afterward.

ENERGIZED

Synonym: Invigorated, activated, stimulated, exhilarated.

What you're saying is you feel energized each time you see that cute little pink bunny commercial?

ENGROSSED

Synonym: Absorbed, occupied, permeated, pervaded, focused.

You were feeling so engrossed in your work, you forgot to pick up the kids and take them to the zoo.

ENGULFED

Synonym: Submerged, inundated, swallowed-up, buried, swamped.

She leaves you feeling engulfed in her problems and then goes skipping off like nothing's wrong?

ENRAGED

Synonym: Angered, infuriated, incensed, provoked, exacerbated.

When you found the letters she had written to him you felt enraged, not realizing they were written years ago?

ENSLAVED

Synonym: Imprisoned, confined, restrained, oppressed, restricted.

You feel enslaved with your grand-children; she just dropped them off, and you haven't seen her for weeks?

ENTANGLED

Synonym: Trapped, cornered, embroiled, caught, raveled.

So you feel entangled in this love triangle, but now you want out?

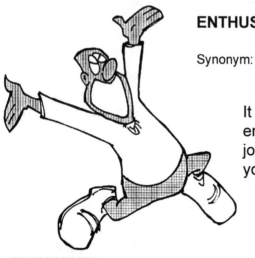

ENTHUSIASTIC

Synonym: Animated, thrilled, titillated, exhilarated.

It sounds like you felt enthusiastic about your new job until you discovered you couldn't do it.

ENTOMBED

Synonym: Imprisoned, buried, confined, incarcerated, trapped.

He's so jealous he won't let you leave the house; you must feel entombed.

ENVIOUS

Synonym: Jealous, greedy, desiring, craving, covetous, wishful.

So you felt envious that other people were invited, and then you lashed out in anger.

EROTIC

Synonym: Sensual, carnal, lewd, indecent, unbridled, lustful, amorous.

Are you telling me that you felt erotic in the skimpy outfit, but he didn't seem to notice?

ESTRANGED

Synonym: Alienated, withdrawn, separated, removed, disunited.

It sounds like you felt estranged when you visited your ex-in-laws on Christmas, and the family seemed cold.

ETHICAL

Synonym: Decent, honest, respectable, moral, humane, noble.

I'm hearing that you felt ethical when you wouldn't release confidential client information to the media, despite the publicity your agency would have received.

EVASIVE

Synonym: Sly, deceitful, misleading, false, dishonest.

You seem to feel evasive every time you're asked how you hope this agency can help you.

EVIL

Synonym: Wicked, sinful, immoral, depraved, corrupt, harmful.

Wishing he would just die and get it over with makes you feel evil, but he's suffered so long?

EXACERBATED

Synonym: Provoked, angered, bothered, annoyed, irritated.

You feel exacerbated; the plumbing is plugged, the heat doesn't work and there's garbage in the halls?

EXCEPTIONAL

Synonym: Rare, unusual, extraordinary, uncommon, special, unmatched.

It sounds like you feel exceptional when you astound coworkers with your memories of cases.

EXCITABLE

Synonym: Irritable, sensitive, impatient, intolerant, hysterical.

It seems you feel highly excitable about the same time each month; could it be hormone related?

EXCITED

Synonym: Stimulated, aroused, delighted, enthusiastic.

You must have felt excited when you won the lottery!

EXHAUSTED

Synonym: Tired, weary, worn, consumed, debilitated.

It sounds like you felt exhausted after walking 5 miles, but also felt a sense of accomplishment.

EXHILARATED

Synonym: Invigorated, inspired, lively, stimulated, enlivened.

I'm hearing that you felt exhilarated when he puts his arms around you, but that intimacy still frightens you a bit?

EXILED

Synonym: Cast out, banished, discarded, ostracized, displaced.

Sounds like you're feeling exiled; you found your stuff in the hall and his stuff in the closet.

EXONERATED

Synonym: Excused, absolved, acquitted, pardoned, freed, vindicated.

Having won your appeal on a technicality makes you feel exonerated, but you're still guilty in the eyes of your friends and family?

EXPERIENCED

Synonym: Skilled, mature, accomplished, able, qualified, masterful.

So, you felt experienced enough to handle the job, but it didn't turn out so well.

EXPLOITED

Synonym: Used, abused, milked, duped.

I think you're saying you felt exploited when you discovered they invited you because you have a nice car.

EXPLOSIVE

Synonym: Violent, uncontrollable, dangerous, eruptive, hysterical.

I'm sensing that you felt explosive when you realized that your friends neglected to warn you about Mexican water?

EXPOSED

Synonym: Uncovered, disclosed, naked, revealed, divulged, unmasked.

So, you felt exposed when the Playboy pictures turned up 15 years later in the tabloids?

EXPRESSIONLESS

Synonym: Dull, blank, mute, empty, vacant, hollow.

I see you felt expressionless as you listened to the litany of crimes committed against your child.

EXPRESSIVE

Synonym: Articulate, eloquent, passionate, artistic, stimulating.

My impression is that you felt expressive dancing nude in the park, but the police didn't agree and arrested you anyway.

FACETIOUS

Synonym: Funny, comical, clever, whimsical, satirical, jesting.

So, you were feeling facetious when you made the remark, but they took you seriously and are all feeling hurt?

FAINT

Synonym: Weak, dizzy, faltering, frail, sickly, unsteady.

You say you're feeling faint; how long has it been since you've eaten?

FAITHFUL

Synonym: Loyal, trustworthy, honorable, devoted, unwavering, sincere.

I hear that you feel faithful in the relationship, but don't feel secure that she can be.

FAITHLESS

Synonym: Skeptical, atheistic, unbelieving, agnostic, dubious.

It sounds like you felt faithless as you listened to your friend describe her beliefs.

FALLIBLE

Synonym: Untrustworthy, deceptive, unreliable, uncertain, frail, imperfect.

So, you felt fallible when you were confronted with the lies you had told?

FALLOW

Synonym: Unused, uncultivated, neglected, unproductive, inactive, dormant.

Raising a family was your choice, but you still feel fallow when you think of the career you left behind.

FAMISHED

Synonym: Hungry, starving, longing for, unnourished.

It sounds like you feel famished for affection, but are unable to get those needs met by being afraid to ask for it.

FANATICAL

Synonym: Obsessed, feverish, enthusiastic, zealous, impassioned.

So, you still feel fanatical about baseball, but your husband doesn't share your interest?

FANTASTIC

Synonym: Whimsical, wonderful, extravagant, outlandish, unconventional.

So, you felt fantastic after the workout, until every muscle in your body began to ache?

FASCINATED

Synonym: Entranced, charmed, captivated, excited, provoked, enticed.

It sounds like you felt fascinated by the mass murderer's story, although it simultaneously repulsed you.

FASCINATING

Synonym: Charming, attractive, enchanting, delightful, engaging.

So, you felt fascinating as you regaled them with your family history, but they seemed bored.

FASHIONABLE

Synonym: Stylish, in vogue, trendy, hot, current, popular.

It seems you felt fashionable in your new hat, but wondered why no other girl at school was wearing one?

FATIGUED

Synonym: Exhausted, weary, tired, weak, listless, feeble.

It sounds like you felt fatigued after the weekend with your nieces and nephews.

FAULTED

Synonym: Blamed, accused, charged, liable, accountable, responsible.

So, you felt faulted in the accident by the police, even though the witnesses testified otherwise.

FAULTLESS

Synonym: Perfect, impeccable, immaculate, without deceit, untainted.

So, you feel faultless in the breakup and feel it was all her fault?

FAVORABLE

Synonym: Approving, agreeable, willing, supportive, helpful, encouraging.

I'm sensing that you felt favorable about the candidate, but your coworkers all shot you down.

FEARFUL

Synonym: Cowardly, cautious, timid, apprehensive, shy.

It sounds like you felt fearful walking down the dark street, but kept your guard up.

FEARLESS

Synonym: Bold, brave, courageous, dashing, daring.

It sounds like you felt fearless rescuing the baby from the burning house, but are quite shaken now.

EEBLE

ynonym: Weak, ineffective, impotent, fragile, puny.

hear you feeling feeble in your ttempts to get your agenda ems heard, and don't know ow to better present them.

EMININE

ynonym: Womanly, gentle, delicate, sensitive, matronly, maidenly.

:ver since high school you've felt feminine inside and are now eady to look into sexual reassignment surgery?

EROCIOUS

ynonym: Fierce, brutish, wild, cruel, savage, violent.

>o, you felt ferocious as you defended your home from the intruders ind now wonder where all that courage came from?

ESTIVE

ynonym: Happy, gay, cheerful, joyous, delighted, rapturous.

hear you were feeling festive in doing the Mexican hat dance in ostume, but wish your boss hadn't taped it.

ETTERED

ynonym: Shackled, hampered, chained, restrained, inhibited, suppressed.

t sounds like you feel fettered by your parents' rules, but are afraid ɔ confront them.

FEVERISH

Synonym: Hot, burning, unstable, infatuated, encompassed.

So, you felt feverish as you slow danced with him and you were amazed to feel such passion?

FICKLE

Synonym: Whimsical, changeable, capricious, unpredictable, faithless, untrue.

I hear that you feel fickle dating three women at once, but aren't sure if you want to stop it.

FIDGETY

Synonym: Restless, nervous, squeamish, uneasy, uncomfortable.

It sounds like you felt fidgety as you waited for the loan officer to render his decision.

FIENDISH

Synonym: Diabolical, wicked, evil, devilish, satanic, barbaric.

I sense that you feel fiendish as you think of ways to get even with them.

FIERCE

Synonym: Ferocious, raging, vicious, bestial, furious, wild, violent.

It sounds like you felt fierce after drinking tequila, but are now embarrassed by your behavior.

ILTHY

ynonym: Dirty, foul, contaminated, polluted, nasty, corrupt.

hear that you felt filthy after the assault and wonder if you'll ever
el clean again.

IRM

ynonym: Convinced, unmovable, settled, unshakable, steady, fixed.

ly impression is that you feel firm in the belief that the impotence
temporary.

IXATED

ynonym: Obsessed, preoccupied, haunted, captivated, plagued, seized.

n sensing that you feel fixated on your goal of finishing school
ven though it seems an endless task?

LABBERGASTED

ynonym: Amazed, astounded, surprised,
           aghast, confounded.

sounds like you felt flabbergasted
hen you saw a platypus on
e porch?

LAKY

ynonym: Silly, wacky, offbeat,
           eccentric, strange.

elling me that you feel flaky
oesn't help much; can you
ll me what kind of pills
ou took?

FLAMBOYANT

Synonym: Ornate, flashy, showy, ostentatious, gaudy.

Would it be accurate to say you felt flamboyant in drag, but regre
stopping by the office dressed that way?

FLATTERED

Synonym: Complemented, praised, lauded, exalted.

I hear you feel flattered by his attention, but aren't sure how to reac
to it.

FLEXIBLE

Synonym: Manageable, pliant, docile, agreeable, accommodating,
                adaptable.

So, you were feeling flexible when you offered to work any shift, and
now they're taking advantage of you?

FLIGHTY

Synonym: Capricious, impulsive, fickle, changeable, whimsical.

So, you were felt flighty when you changed your destination three
times before deciding on your first choice?

FLIPPANT

Synonym: Rude, impudent, insulting, impertinent, smart.

Are you sure an obscene gesture was appropriate just because you
were feeling flippant?

FOOLISH

Synonym: Stupid, dumb, insane, absurd, preposterous, ridiculous.

Your dad warned you what you were getting into; now you feel foolish that you didn't listen?

FORGOTTEN

Synonym: Abandoned, lost, deserted, neglected, shunned, forsaken.

I'm hearing that you feel forgotten because no one remembered your birthday?

FORLORN

Synonym: Forsaken, miserable, abandoned, forgotten.

It sounds like you felt forlorn when your parents left you with a relative and went to New York for a week.

FORSAKEN

Synonym: Destitute, deserted, neglected, abandoned, forlorn.

As he rode off into the sunset, you felt forsaken, but after all, it was only a movie.

FRAGILE

Synonym: Weak, breakable, tender, brittle, delicate, frail.

Just thinking that he may someday hurt you makes you feel fragile?

FRAMED

Synonym: Set up, cheated, betrayed, deceived, crossed.

It sounds like you felt framed when the computer blew, and everyone implied it was your fault.

FRANK

Synonym: Candid, open, sincere, direct, outspoken, free, easy, forthright.

I get the feeling that you felt frank as you expressed yourself, but now she won't speak to you?

FRANTIC

Synonym: Mad, wild, insane, crazy, excited, furious, angry.

I hear you felt frantic when you lost sight of your child in the store.

FRAUDULENT

Synonym: Deceitful, dishonest, treacherous, sneaky, false, tricky, untruthful.

Each time you sell another one of those vacuum cleaners you feel fraudulent, but you're good at it?

FREAKISH

Synonym: Abnormal, disfigured, odd, strange, ugly, unusual.

So, you felt freakish leaving the beauty shop with your new hairdo, but your friends think it's great?

FREED

Synonym: Liberated, emancipated, discharged, released, extricated.

It sounds like you felt freed the day your divorce was granted, but now you aren't so sure?

FRETFUL

Synonym: Irritable, cross, peevish, ill-tempered, touchy, excitable.

It seems like you felt fretful while waiting for the test results, but now are relieved to know you're healthy?

FRIENDLY

Synonym: Helpful, sympathetic, kind, caring, approachable, amicable.

So, you felt friendly toward the stranded motorist, but she seemed afraid to talk to you.

FRIGHTENED

Synonym: Scared, intimidated, afraid, terrorized, startled.

It sounds like you were frightened by the earthquake since you had just moved from the East Coast.

FRIGID

Synonym: Unresponsive, undersexed, unloved, cold, indifferent.

I'm sensing that you have felt frigid toward him ever since you first suspected he is having an affair.

FROLICSOME

Synonym: Happy, playful, merry, jovial, whimsical.

You mooned the traffic cop because you felt frolicsome, but don't think he'll be able to identify you in a line-up?

FRUGAL

Synonym: Thrifty, prudent, careful, parsimonious, economical.

I'm hearing that you feel frugal with the family budget, but your husband spends lavishly.

FRUSTRATED

Synonym: Defeated, disappointed, subdued, beaten, crushed, conquered.

It sounds like you feel frustrated with your friend's inability to be on time, when you are always prompt.

FULFILLED

Synonym: Satisfied, accomplished, perfected, actualized, consummated.

So, you feel fulfilled having three children, but your wife wants more?

FURIOUS

Synonym: Enraged, angry, raging, fierce, intense, violent, turbulent.

I hear that you felt furious when the doctor kept you waiting over 45 minutes, so you left without seeing him and now you have to go back?

FUTILE

Synonym: Useless, fruitless, unproductive, ineffective, impracticable.

Are you saying you felt futile in your attempt to resuscitate your neighbor, and now you feel guilty that you didn't try hard enough?

GENEROUS

Synonym: Beneficent, charitable, unselfish, philanthropic, bountiful.

Every time you encounter someone needy you feel generous, but now you're finding you barely have enough for yourself.

GHASTLY

Synonym: Offensive, hideous, frightful, abhorrent, horrible, frightening.

I get the feeling that you felt ghastly at the beach in a bathing suit until you saw women twice your size in string bikinis.

GLAMOROUS

Synonym: Fascinating, charming, charismatic, alluring, dazzling, bewitching.

I'm hearing that you felt glamorous in the sequined evening gown, but arrived to find everyone in jeans.

GLOOMY

Synonym: Downhearted, depressed, morose, sad.

Are you saying thunderstorms always leave you feeling gloomy?

GLOWING

Synonym: Radiant, enthusiastic, bright, lustrous, gleaming.

It sounds like you felt glowing after spending two hours in the tanning booth.

GRACEFUL

Synonym: Elegant, dexterous, nimble, balanced, exquisite, rhythmic.

I'm hearing that you felt graceful as you flitted up the stage steps to accept the award, but then knocked over the podium?

GRACIOUS

Synonym: Polite, courteous, merciful, charitable, loving, kind, amiable.

So you're saying that you felt gracious when you offered to have the party, but then discovered the invitations went out to everyone you can't stand?

GREAT

Synonym: Eminent, noble, grand, renowned, celebrated, magnificent.

I'll bet you felt great when you finally graduated after all those years of part-time study.

GUARDED

Synonym: Careful, cautious, watchful, observant, attentive.

Every time we start talking about how he treats the kids you seem to feel very guarded.

GUILTY

Synonym: Condemned, responsible, at fault, wrong, blameworthy, liable.

I'm hearing that you felt guilty leaving on vacation the day before your aunt's funeral.

GULLIBLE

Synonym: Naive, innocent, trusting, inexperienced, simple.

You feel so gullible falling for that old story about having to work late?

HAGGARD

Synonym: Weak, worn-out, gaunt, tiresome, beaten, exhausted.

It sounds like you were feeling haggard as you flipped on the country music and flopped on the couch.

HANDICAPPED

Synonym: Crippled, impeded, challenged, disadvantaged, encumbered.

I'm hearing that you felt handicapped the moment you realized he was a pool shark, but you shot a few games anyway.

HAPPY

Synonym: Merry, joyous, cheerful, delighted, gay, jolly, jovial, content.

Just thinking about the fact that in two more weeks you'll be on your way to the coast for the summer makes you feel happy.

HARASSED

Synonym: Bothered, attacked, annoyed, irritated, teased, troubled.

I'm hearing that you felt harassed by the obscene phone calls, but the police wouldn't do anything.

HEARTLESS

Synonym: Ruthless, savage, cruel, insensitive, brutal, ferocious.

It sounds like you felt heartless when you cut the employees' vacation time, but the budget left you no choice?

HIDEOUS

Synonym: Ugly, grotesque, shocking, frightful, repulsive, offensive.

The burns from the accident make you feel hideous, but the doctors say you should heal OK?

HOMICIDAL

Synonym: Murderous, destructive, lethal, violent, criminal, maniacal.

You say it actually makes you feel homicidal when you think of how badly he cheated you?

HONORED

Synonym: Respected, praised, celebrated, distinguished, important.

So you feel honored each time you see your picture next to the award, but disgusted with the two percent raise?

HOPEFUL

Synonym: Optimistic, expectant, assured, sanguine.

I guess you felt hopeful when you heard the doctor say he thinks it is benign.

HOPELESS

Synonym: Despondent, pessimistic, cynical, despairing, disconsolate.

I think I hear you saying you began feeling hopeless when the third bill collector called.

HORNY

Synonym: Excited, sensual, aroused, lewd, lecherous.

You were feeling horny when she got home, but she wanted to put the groceries away first?

HOSTILE

Synonym: Antagonistic, hateful, opposed, unfriendly.

It seems you felt hostile when your co-worker received the promotion.

HUMANE

Synonym: Kind, benevolent, understanding, caring, sympathetic, gentle.

Each time you find another stray you feel humane, but seventeen cats does seem a little excessive.

HUMILIATED

Synonym: Ashamed, embarrassed, disgraced, mortified, humbled.

So you felt humiliated when your mother told the story of you wetting your pants in school.

HUMOROUS

Synonym: Witty, clever, comical, funny, entertaining.

What you're saying is, you were feeling humorous all evening, but the next morning your boyfriend wouldn't even talk to you?

HUNGRY

Synonym: Starved, craving, unsatisfied, famished.

You're feeling hungry for affection, but she won't even let you near her anymore?

HUNTED

Synonym: Pursued, stalked, chased, hounded, trailed, dogged.

You felt hunted when you saw his car parked down the block, ran inside, and slammed the door?

HURT

Synonym: Injured, wounded,
bruised, damaged,
mauled, agonized,
insulted.

You were feeling really hurt when she said your nose was too big, your eyes were too far apart, and your mouth was too small.

IMPLICATED

Synonym: Involved, suspect, indicated, connected.

Just his cold, icy stare was enough to leave you feeling implicated.

IMPORTANT

Synonym: Significant, illustrious, distinguished, remarkable, powerful.

Being made supervisor made you feel important, but it wasn't enough to get the respect of the staff?

INDEBTED

Synonym: Obligated, responsible, grateful, thankful, bound.

So you felt indebted to your folks for all they have done, but now you have no life of your own?

INDECISIVE

Synonym: Uncertain, doubtful, irresolute, vague, wavering.

She says she won't wait any longer, but you still feel indecisive about the wedding.

INDENTURED

Synonym: Enslaved, indebted, obligated, grateful, bound, strapped.

Taking charity makes you feel indentured; you can always make a donation when you're back on your feet.

INDIGNANT

Synonym: Angry, insulted, upset, displeased, resentful, offended, annoyed.

Each time I ask about your part in the break-up you start feeling indignant; have you noticed that?

INDUSTRIOUS

Synonym: Laborious, diligent, active, busy, useful.

It seems that volunteering at 'Habitat for Humanity' leaves you feeling industrious and philanthropic.

INEXCUSABLE

Synonym: Wrong, indefensible, unforgivable, reprehensible.

It seems inexcusable that you forgot your anniversary, and she's quick to agree?

INFATUATED

Synonym: Charmed, fascinated, intoxicated, seduced, beguiled, bewitched.

You felt infatuated by the bright lights and fast life, but now you would give anything to be back home on the farm?

INFERIOR

Synonym: Second-rate, poor, subordinate, mediocre, secondary, common.

Your sister's cutting remarks always made you feel inferior, and you're only now realizing the long lasting effects?

INFURIATED

Synonym: Angered, enraged, aggravated, provoked, incensed.

So you felt infuriated that this teenage girl couldn't enter the left turn lane properly and really lost it?

INJURED

Synonym: Wounded, hurt, damaged, bruised, scarred, disabled.

You're saying that you felt injured when you weren't invited to the wedding, even though you wouldn't have gone?

INQUISITIVE

Synonym: Curious, interested, questioning, intrusive, speculative.

Sounds like you're feeling inquisitive about the prescription drugs you found in your wife's purse?

INSPIRED

Synonym: Motivated, encouraged, driven, aroused, stirred, ecstatic.

You say you feel inspired by 'voices' - they're telling you to jump?

INSULTED

Synonym: Cursed, humiliated, slandered, offended, hurt, shamed.

I'm sorry you feel insulted by my suggestion, but you say others have told you the same thing?

INTIMIDATED

Synonym: Afraid, frightened,
             fearful, threatened,
             scared.

You say these kids milling around the street corner have you feeling intimidated - you are wondering what they are up to?

INTROVERTED

Synonym: Shy, self-centered, bashful, egocentric, indrawn.

They make you feel introverted just because you would rather listen than talk?

INVISIBLE

Synonym: Transparent, intangible, obscure, neglected, ignored.

So, the frantic crowd at the blue light special made you feel invisible?

INVULNERABLE

Synonym: Invincible, indestructible, secure.

You're telling me you were feeling invulnerable as the speedometer crept past 100 m.p.h. and now two of your best friends are dead.

IRRITABLE

Synonym: Annoyed, sensitive, excitable, touchy, ill-tempered.

Without the cigarettes you feel irritable, yet you know they're killing you?

IRRITATED

Synonym: Angry, upset, troubled, disturbed, hurt, provoked.

You say you're feeling irritated that I won't tell you what you should do; don't you think it would be better to come from within <u>you</u>?

JEALOUS

Synonym: Envious, suspicious, possessive, begrudging, mistrustful.

Even though he has never given you any reason, you feel jealous inside?

JUBILANT

Synonym: Ecstatic, overjoyed, rejoicing, delightful.

I hear that you're feeling jubilant that your pen pal finally is coming to meet you; now you're wishing you had sent her your own picture.

JUMPY

Synonym: Excited, nervous, restless, agitated, trembling.

You feel jumpy with the new medication, but can't function at all without it?

JUSTIFIED

Synonym: Defensible, proper, right, reasonable, permissible.

You say they don't pay you enough and that's why you felt justified embezzling the money?

LACKADAISICAL

Synonym: Dull, lazy, unmotivated, listless, slow, unfocused, inattentive.

As soon as you get to work you start feeling lackadaisical, but come alive at five?

LISTLESS

Synonym: Lazy, sluggish, weary, tired, apathetic, lethargic, drowsy.

Ever since he left you, you've been feeling listless and you can't even leave the house?

LOGICAL

Synonym: Rational, reasonable, cerebral, sensible, coherent.

I hear you saying you felt quite logical, but she was looking for feeling.

LONELY

Synonym: Forlorn, isolated, solitary, deserted, abandoned, rejected.

I'm hearing that you sometimes feel lonely, yet you feel it is the price you pay for independence.

LOST

Synonym: Helpless, alone, feeble, abandoned, astray.

It sounds like you felt lost and didn't know which way to turn for direction.

LOUSY

Synonym: Horrible, infested, disliked, sickly, unpopular.

It seems like you felt lousy when you had the mangy, rabid dog put to sleep.

LOVED

Synonym: Cherished, valued, adored, treasured, beloved, desired.

I'm hearing that you have never truly felt loved, in spite of the fact that you have been told so.

LUCKY

Synonym: Fortunate, hopeful, blessed, magical, prosperous.

You're telling me you felt lucky when you went to the track, and now you're looking for a food voucher.

LUSTFUL

Synonym: Sensual, desirous, longing, wanting, lascivious, lecherous.

Each time she leans over your desk you feel lustful; she's becoming an obsession with you.

LYRICAL

Synonym: Poetic, musical, melodious, expressive, emotional, rhythmic.

You're saying you felt lyrical singing Elvis songs at the bar, until you saw the video when you sobered up.

MAGNETIC

Synonym: Attractive, alluring, charming, irresistible, captivating, fascinating.

The way the kids warm up to you makes you feel magnetic; they want you to coach their team?

MAGNIFICENT

Synonym: Luxurious, glorious, noble, brilliant, grand, great, exalted.

When you got called for the audition you felt magnificent, but now you found out you'll have to give up school.

MAJESTIC

Synonym: Grand, royal, supreme, noble, dignified, exalted.

You felt majestic standing on the rim of the canyon; you could sense the presence of God?

MALFORMED

Synonym: Crippled, deformed, abnormal, distorted, grotesque, twisted.

You actually feel malformed just because you're shorter than the other kids?

MALICIOUS

Synonym: Revengeful, spiteful, evil, vicious, hateful, hostile, bitter.

Have you considered that this malicious feeling can only lead to more trouble?

MARKED

Synonym: Branded, labeled, scared, stamped, imprinted.

None of the girls will go out with you anymore; you somehow feel marked, but don't know why?

MARVELOUS

Synonym: Fabulous, miraculous, astonishing, unusual, wonderful, supernatural.

You say you felt marvelous when Marvin mailed you the mechanical mechanism that played melodious music; do you always talk this way?

MELANCHOLY

Synonym: Sad, dreary, depressed, unhappy, dispirited, despairing.

Now that the project is over you just feel melancholy; you thought you'd feel elated?

MELLOW

Synonym: Mature, cultured, adult, cultivated, grown.

When you finally earned your degree, you felt mellow, but all your dad could say was: "It's about time".

MIFFED

Synonym: Provoked, angry, offended, annoyed, pestered, bothered.

So you feel miffed that your brother won't pay you the money he owes you?

MILITANT

Synonym: Aggressive, combative, belligerent, offensive, resistant.

Watching the documentary only made you feel militant all over again; you are not satisfied with the progress of the last 30 years.

MINDLESS

Synonym: Thoughtless, inconsiderate, careless, neglectful, negligent.

Realizing what you had done made you feel mindless; someone could have really been hurt.

MISCHIEVOUS

Synonym: Playful, naughty, whimsical, prankish, spirited.

You were only feeling mischievous when you booby trapped the outhouse, but she was OK when they pulled her out?

MISERABLE

Synonym: Sick, ill, troubled, distressed, suffering, wretched, pitiful.

When you realized he was in there with another woman, you felt miserable?

MISGUIDED

Synonym: Misled, wrong, deceived, mistaken, confused.

Looking back at many of the things your father taught you leaves you feeling misguided, but he did teach you to think for yourself?

MORBID

Synonym: Sickly, gloomy, gruesome, morose, demented, despondent.

Having lived through it, it makes you feel morbid that they are selling tapes of the Holocaust on TV.

MORONIC

Synonym: Stupid, brainless, irrational, ridiculous.

Struggling with the exam for two hours only to find you were in the wrong room must have made you feel moronic.

MYSTIFIED

Synonym: Deceived, perplexed, tricked, enchanted, bewildered, confused.

So you felt mystified as she slowly turned the cards, describing the hidden meaning of each one?

NAIVE

Synonym: Innocent, inexperienced, simple, unsophisticated, trusting, unpretentious.

Now you feel naive thinking he could have possibly had your interests in mind.

NAUGHTY

Synonym: Mischievous, wanton, disobedient, playful, spirited.

Sometimes you feel naughty and want to play but he just can't seem to loosen up?

NAUSEOUS

Synonym: Disgusting, revolting, sickening, repulsive, offensive.

Whenever you enter the plant, you start feeling nauseous; perhaps we could call OSHA?

NEEDED

Synonym: Wanted, desired, required, adequate, necessary.

It makes you feel needed when she drops off the kids, but then you found she just goes home and goes back to bed?

NERVOUS

Synonym: Excitable, sensitive, apprehensive, annoyed, agitated.

I can tell you're feeling nervous about the exam; when will the results be available?

NOSTALGIC

Synonym: Sentimental, homesick, lonely, remorseful, regretful, lonesome.

Looking at the family album makes you feel nostalgic; you miss those good old times?

NUMB

Synonym: Unfeeling, dull, paralyzed, callous, indifferent, apathetic.

When you heard the charges against him, you felt numb; perhaps you suspect he may be guilty?

OBSCURE

Synonym: Vague, ambiguous, dubious, mysterious, concealed, questionable.

You feel obscure about the memories of last night, but somehow don't think it went very well.

OBSESSED

Synonym: Troubled, plagued, haunted, captivated, overpowered, preoccupied.

Each night before you can sleep, you feel obsessed to drive by his house?

OLD

Synonym: Aged, elderly, matured, feeble, exhausted, deficient, decrepit.

It sounds like you started feeling old when you heard Mick Jagger was a grandfather?

OPPRESSED

Synonym: Abused, enslaved, bound, mistreated, smothered, suppressed.

For years you've felt oppressed; you feel he's denied you your life?

OPTIMISTIC

Synonym: Trusting, hopeful, confident, faithful, enthusiastic, assured.

When you submitted the manuscript, you were feeling optimistic; but now after three rejections you've lost hope?

OSTRACIZED

Synonym: Banished, exiled, expelled, ignored, segregated, evicted, excluded.

Now that you've decided to admit you're gay, you feel ostracized by your friends and family.

OUTSTANDING

Synonym: Important, great, superb, excellent, noble, distinguished.

You felt outstanding when they called your name; you were so proud to be nominated.

OUTWITTED

Synonym: Deceived, tricked, befuddled, bewildered, outsmarted.

It sounds like you feel outwitted, but you still feel you're the best woman for the office?

OVERCOME

Synonym: Beaten, whipped, defeated, conquered, overwhelmed, subdued.

So you felt overcome to learn that on top of everything else, you let your coverage lapse.

OVERCONFIDENT

Synonym: Careless, reckless, attentive, unmindful, regardless, unthinking.

So you felt overconfident when you took on the project - that has gotten you in trouble before?

OVERCRITICAL

Synonym: Harsh, severe, insensitive, domineering, tyrannical, oppressive.

Now you're feeling overcritical of your son because he is gay, and wish you could find him to beg his forgiveness.

OVERCROWDED

Synonym: Congested, uncomfortable, squeezed, overpopulated.

It sounds like you feel overcrowded in elevators and such; that's when you panic?

OVEREXCITED

Synonym: Hyperactive, restless, overestimated, incited.

Are you saying that it's when your child feels overexcited that he's most prone to the seizures?

OVEREXTENDED

Synonym: Over-committed, in debt, indentured.

I hear that you're feeling overextended with a job, school, volunteer work, and a family; let's talk about priorities.

OVERINDULGENT

Synonym: Lenient, tolerant, permissive, liberal.

You say you feel overindulgent when you let the kids run all over you, but now things are completely out of control?

OVERJOYED

Synonym: Thrilled, inspired, electrified, excited, overwhelmed, enraptured.

So you felt overjoyed when she won the scholarship; it was a dream come true?

OVERLOOKED

Synonym: Neglected, ignored, left out, bypassed, isolated, segregated, omitted.

If you feel overlooked each time there's an opportunity, how can you ask the boss about it?

OVERRATED

Synonym: Exaggerated, unsatisfactory, disappointing.

It sounds like you feel overrated by her praise, yet you've accomplished so much more with her by your side.

OVERRUN

Synonym: Trampled, abused, ignored, neglected.

You must have felt overrun when you told the kids to break up the party and go home, and they just laughed at you?

OVERSHADOWED

Synonym: Diminished, ignored, dominated, belittled, depreciated.

So you are feeling overshadowed by your big brother; has he always been your Dad's hero?

OVERWHELMED

Synonym: Conquered, defeated, crushed, ruined, smashed, subjugated.

Looking at the stack of bills and the empty checkbook must have you feeling overwhelmed?

OVERWORKED

Synonym: Tired, exhausted, overburdened, spent.

I hear you were already feeling overworked when the boss handed you another assignment.

PAINFUL

Synonym: Aching, bruised, hurting, tormented, grievous.

You're saying it feels painful to see the starving faces on TV; but even if they are fed, each year there seems to be more?

PAMPERED

Synonym: Spoiled, indulged, coddled, babied.

So even though you think he would give you anything he could, you are not accustomed to feeling pampered?

PANIC-STRICKEN

Synonym: Terrified, hysterical, frantic, afraid, delirious, frazzled.

You felt panic-stricken as he tried to pull you into the car, but managed to struggle free and find a phone.

PARALYZED

Synonym: Immobile, disabled, helpless, numb.

Do you feel paralyzed knowing some of your ideas may be lucrative business opportunities, but you're trapped with you current responsibilities?

PARDONABLE

Synonym: Forgivable, excusable, absolvable, innocent.

So you are feeling pardonable, but you have beaten her before, and each time it has been worse?

PAROCHIAL

Synonym: Biased, prejudiced, narrow-minded, shallow, conservative.

Even if you do feel parochial about your education, it is never too late to open your mind to new concepts.

PARSIMONIOUS

Synonym: Tight, greedy, selfish, stingy, frugal.

To say this politely, you're feeling parsimonious, but this is Detroit and kids need winter coats; do you agree?

PARTIAL

Synonym: Prejudiced, biased, unfair, favoring, inclined.

So you feel partial to red and black and think that if you have to paint your own room, you should be able to choose the colors?

PASSE

Synonym: Out-moded, old-fashioned, obsolete, antiquated, unfashionable, out-of-date.

If you feel passe about your marketing ideas, perhaps it time to bring in a consultant?

PASSIONATE

Synonym: Romantic, intense, loving, stimulating, inspiring.

So you felt passionate as you watched the Phantom sing to Christine, and wonder why it is difficult to be emotional in your own relationships?

PASSIVE

Synonym: Lifeless, dull, inactive, indifferent, inert, resigned.

Because the meetings are nothing more than semantical gymnastics, you are always left feeling passive and bored.

PATERNAL

Synonym: Fatherly, patrimonial, nurturing, caring, parental, protective.

In your words, you were feeling paternal as the Little League coach and the sexual abuse charges make you feel suicidal.

PATHETIC

Synonym: Pitiful, miserable, dismal, bleak, sorrowful, tearful, wretched.

Now you are feeling pathetic knowing that after an eight-month dry spell you went out and drank last night.

PATIENT

Synonym: Enduring, unwavering, composed, meek, tolerant, submissive.

As Grandma regaled your friends with her medical problems for the 100th time, you felt patient and kind for listening?

PATRIOTIC

Synonym: Devoted, dedicated, nationalistic, civic-minded, loyal.

I'm hearing you say you felt patriotic each time you flew a mission, but now the thought of torn bodies haunts you?

PATRONIZING

Synonym: Condescending, polite, accommodating.

So you're only feeling patronizing when you go along with his ideas; inside you're outraged that your career was not even discussed.

PEACEFUL

Synonym: Calm, comfortable, at rest, mild, tranquil, serene, quiet.

I'm hearing you feel so peaceful when you wake and find her lying next to you.

PERFECT

Synonym: Flawless, untainted, excellent, whole, pure, immaculate, impeccable.

So you felt perfect with candles, music, and dinner and she never showed; she didn't even call?

PERKY

Synonym: Spunky, cheery, brisk, lively, alert.

I hear you say you felt perky when he arrived; perhaps he wasn't in the mood for perky?

PERMISSIVE

Synonym: Tolerant, agreeable, lenient, easy, indifferent.

What I think you're saying is, you feel permissive when you're alone with him and never think of all the talk about safe sex.

PERSECUTED

Synonym: Harassed, tormented, tortured, victimized, abused, tyrannized.

So you felt persecuted as the defense attorney badgered you, and all you wanted to do was put a felon behind bars.

PERSONABLE

Synonym: Friendly, agreeable, pleasant, amiable, attractive, charming.

Because you had been forewarned about her family, you were able to feel personable and relaxed when you met them?

PERSUADED

ynonym: Convinced, impelled, seduced, lured, motivated, influenced.

So you felt persuaded because everyone else was doing it, but you're still having hallucinations occasionally?

PERSUASIVE

ynonym: Convincing, alluring, seductive, impelling, stimulating, effective.

So you felt persuasive when you recommended therapy, only to find out she never followed through?

PERTURBED

ynonym: Distressed, angry, annoyed, confused, disordered, restless, troubled.

It sounds like you felt perturbed when you came home to a mess, after asking the kids to clean it up.

PERVERSE

ynonym: Delinquent, wicked, corrupt, degenerate, deprived, debased.

You say you feel perverse concerning the thoughts you're having; can you tell me about them?

PERVERTED

ynonym: Corrupt, deviate, wicked, depraved, degenerate.

Although your boyfriend pressured you to go to the topless bar, you now feel perverted and angry with yourself.

PESSIMISTIC

Synonym: Cynical, gloomy, dismal, discouraging, melancholy, despairing.

You say you're feeling pessimistic that he can ever conquer his alcohol problem; perhaps you're finally facing the truth?

PETRIFIED

Synonym: Terrorized, frightened, scared, alarmed, intimidated, afraid.

It sounds like you feel petrified that she may actually kill herself this time.

PETTY

Synonym: Small, insignificant, unimportant, trivial, shallow, weak.

Looking back at some of the arguments you've had now makes you feel petty?

PHILANTHROPIC

Synonym: Benevolent, generous, liberal, kind, humane, charitable.

You were feeling philanthropic when you wrote the check, only to discover the funds were misused?

PIGHEADED

Synonym: Stubborn, obstinate, difficult, unreasonable, headstrong, resolute.

Now you feel pigheaded; if you would have invested, you would be rich?

PIOUS

Synonym: Religious, divine, holy, devout, hallowed, sacred, ecclesiastical.

Your attempts to spread the Word make you feel pious, but so many shun you?

PITILESS

Synonym: Heartless, callous, unfeeling, unmerciful, cold, indifferent, hardhearted.

It sounds like you feel pitiless towards the homeless, like somehow they are responsible for their own condition.

PLAYFUL

Synonym: Frolicsome, humorous, spirited, happy, comical, whimsical.

You felt playful as you tickled him, but he was not in the mood.

PLEASANT

Synonym: Warm, friendly, agreeable, gracious, gentle, cheerful, mild.

So you feel pleasant when you are with your husband, but you want passion and lust?

POPULAR

Synonym: Well-liked, attractive, famous, in demand, familiar, embraced.

For a while you enjoyed feeling popular with the boys, but now you are discouraged by their motives.

POSSESSED

Synonym: Mad, crazed, insane, bewitched, entranced, charmed, enchanted.

I hear you feel possessed when the voices begin; what do they say to you?

POTENT

Synonym: Powerful, strong, vigorous, mighty, influential, dominant.

You say you felt potent when you volunteered for crisis work, but now you wonder how much good you're doing.

POWERLESS

Synonym: Weak, feeble, impotent, helpless, trapped, incompetent.

So you felt powerless as the flames engulfed the building, and will always wonder if you could have saved him?

PRAGMATIC

Synonym: Realistic, utilitarian, logical, reasonable.

So it felt pragmatic to suggest the abortion, but you immediately recognized her discomfort and disapproval.

PRANKISH

Synonym: Mischievous, playful, naughty, disobedient.

When you tossed him the firecracker, you were feeling prankish; how do you feel now?

PRECARIOUS

Synonym: Dubious, endangered, at risk, cautious.

I hear you saying you feel precarious driving your Pinto on the Interstates?

PREJUDICED

Synonym: Biased, intolerant, narrow-minded, conditioned, opinionated.

You're saying you were surprised to feel prejudiced toward the client because you normally are non-judgmental.

PREOCCUPIED

Synonym: Obsessed, entranced, absorbed, enraptured, distracted.

It seems as though you have been feeling preoccupied with thoughts of suicide.

PREPOSTEROUS

Synonym: Absurd, stupid, fantastic, impossible, outrageous.

I hear you feel preposterous in the chicken costume, but you also said you have to work.

PROMINENT

Synonym: Famous, conspicuous, notable.

You felt prominent when you saw your name in the headlines, but it seems to have cost you your privacy.

PROSPEROUS

Synonym: Rich, well-off, successful, wealthy.

I hear you saying you felt prosperous taking her to such a fine restaurant until you came out and found your car repossessed.

PROUD

Synonym: Honorable, self-respecting, confident, self-assured, reputable.

So you felt proud when you finally earned your degree, but now they are telling you it is not going to make any difference in your career?

PROVOKED

Synonym: Angered, infuriated, troubled, enraged, tormented, incensed.

So you felt provoked, but the truth is that it is abuse and you do need help.

PURE

Synonym: Untouched, virgin, spotless, clean, chaste, celibate, innocent.

You say you felt pure telling him you were still a virgin, but he said, "At my age, that sounds like a hassle."

PUZZLED

Synonym: Confused, befuddled, perplexed, doubtful, bewildered, mystified.

They are bringing in all new computers and you feel puzzled; you just learned about the old ones.

QUARRELSOME

Synonym: Argumentative, combative, excitable, irritable, petulant.

It makes you feel quarrelsome just being in the same meeting with her, because she rambles on and on?

QUEASY

Synonym: Uneasy, squeamish, ill, uncomfortable, sick, uneasy.

So you feel queasy just thinking about amusement parks, but you are intent on proving yourself to your kids?

QUIET

Synonym: Calm, silent, peaceful, restful, content, reserved, still, mute.

It sounds like sometimes you just feel quiet and content, and many interpret that as being unsociable.

RADIANT

Synonym: Bright, illuminating, energizing, brilliant.

It sounds like you felt radiant on your return from your trip to Cherynobl and then found out why you got such a good deal?

RADICAL

Synonym: Revolutionary, rebellious, fanatical, militant, riotous, insurgent.

You say drugs make you feel radical; I'm not sure we share the same definition of that.

READY

Synonym: Eager, enthusiastic, prepared, equipped, able, anxious.

You felt ready for anything until she pointed to the mechanical bull?

REASSURED

Synonym: Comforted, encouraged, consoled, confident, convinced.

Once he took the time to explain why he needed the money, you felt reassured he would be coming back?

REBELLIOUS

Synonym: Hostile, violent, aggressive, lawless, dissident, revolutionary.

All through high school you felt rebellious; no one ever tried to understand you?

REFLECTIVE

Synonym: Thoughtful, contemplative, studious, observant, considerate.

Reading the great philosophers inspires you to feel reflective; it is an escape from everyday life?

REFORMED

Synonym: Renewed, enlightened, corrected, improved, redeemed, rectified.

When you got released you felt reformed, but still no one wants to take a chance hiring you?

RELAXED

Synonym: Comfortable, calm, serene, carefree, easy, sedate, unencumbered.

You seem to be feeling much more relaxed than when we first started talking; are you comfortable with your plan?

RELIABLE

Synonym: Trustworthy, dependable, faithful, honest, reasonable, irrefutable.

So you feel reliable always being there for him, but are starting to wonder what is in it for you?

RELIEVED

Synonym: Comforted, calmed, consoled, soothed, relaxed, satisfied.

It sounds like you felt relieved when you finally found the men's room?

RELIGIOUS

Synonym: Pious, godly, faithful, spiritual, moral, holy, unearthly.

You say you started to feel religious as they backed you into the alley -- something you had not felt in years?

RELUCTANT

Synonym: Withholding, disinclined, uncertain, opposed, remiss.

I'm hearing you feel reluctant to do anything else for her even though she is your daughter, because she has cheated you so many times before.

REMORSEFUL

Synonym: Sorry, regretful, penitent, repentant, contrite, grievous.

It sounds like you feel remorseful each time you sneak off to be with him, but yet you keep doing it.

REPREHENSIBLE

Synonym: Guilty, blamable, culpable, wicked, objectionable.

Your marriage has been solid for years, and now you feel reprehensible about your feelings for another woman?

RESENTMENT

Synonym: Anger, hostility, displeasure, bitterness, hatred, animosity.

She only cheated on you once, but it was enough that you will always feel resentment?

RESIGNED

Synonym: Passive, submissive, humble, given up, docile, indifferent.

It sounds like you feel resigned to the fact that you will always have to work for a living when you would like more time to be creative.

RESILIENT

Synonym: Flexible, elastic, recoverable.

You feel resilient; you think you can bounce back from losing your job in the rubber factory.

RESOLUTE

Synonym: Determined, serious, stubborn, persistent, uncompromising.

You sound resolute in your decision to divorce her, but you hate the thought of being alone.

RESOURCEFUL

Synonym: Clever, ingenious, capable, intelligent, astute, original.

It sounds like you felt resourceful when you set up the credit card scam; now you have 6 to 8 years to think about it.

RESPECTABLE

Synonym: Honorable, upright, decent, virtuous, admirable, proper.

Your completely new life has you feeling respectable, but you live in fear that your past might catch up with you?

RESTLESS

Synonym: Uneasy, disturbed, agitated, anxious, jumpy, nervous, flustered.

Since you left rehab you seem to feel restless and unsure of how to fill your free time?

RESTRAINED

Synonym: Controlled, disciplined, repressed, blocked, limited, obstructed.

It sounds like you wish you were more verbally expressive, but you feel restrained by old fears of rejection.

RETICENT

Synonym: Quiet, reserved, private, shy, modest, composed, sedate.

You're finding yourself at ease with this man, although you have usually felt too reticent to get involved with anyone?

REVENGEFUL

Synonym: Vindictive, hateful, ruthless, vengeful, spiteful, malevolent.

You said yourself, feeling revengeful only makes you suffer.

REVERENT

Synonym: Respectful, venerating, religious, courteous, considerate.

You felt reverent entering the temple even though you are not Jewish.

RIDICULOUS

Synonym: Absurd, silly, funny, preposterous, foolish, humorous.

So your fear of clowns sometimes makes you feel ridiculous, especially when no one will take you seriously?

ROMANTIC

Synonym: Enchanted, passionate, loving, affectionate, charming.

Feeling romantic toward this new man frightens you because you have been hurt before?

ROTTEN

Synonym: Offensive, polluted, corrupt, spoiled, disgusting.

When everyone got food poisoning at your barbecue, you must have felt rotten.

ROWDY

Synonym: Disorderly, destructive, hostile, aggressive, wild, foolhardy.

You say you were only feeling rowdy because of the beer, but the judge called it aggravated assault?

RUTHLESS

Synonym: Tyrannical, cruel, heartless, unmerciful, cold, mean, pitiless.

You feel ruthless repossessing your daughter's car, but if you don't, the bank will.

SACRED

Synonym: Holy, saintly, religious, pious, pure, heavenly, ordained.

You are saying you felt sacred near the shrine in your yard and cannot believe the vandals could desecrate it?

SACRILEGIOUS

Synonym: Sinful, blasphemous, wicked, evil, ungodly, profane, impious.

You are saying you felt sacrilegious in church when you realized your mind was on sex and you had not heard a word?

SAD

Synonym: Unhappy, sorrowful, anguished, hopeless, melancholy, dejected.

It makes you feel sad to see your parents losing their friends to illness and death.

SADISTIC

Synonym: Cruel, brutal, vicious, depraved, wicked, degenerate, gross.

Raised by a father with so much hate still makes you feel sadistic occasionally, but you fight it all the time!

SAFE

Synonym: Protected, secure, guarded, preserved, invulnerable, sheltered.

You feel safe when he holds you and assures you; you wish he would do it more often.

SANCTIMONIOUS

Synonym: False, lying, deceptive, hypocritical, bigoted, insincere.

Each time you get up to read the Gospel to the congregation you feel sanctimonious, however you have some other things in your life you have to clean up.

SARCASTIC

Synonym: Offensive, vicious, scornful, insulting, mocking, hostile, cynical.

When you made the comment, you felt sarcastic; now you regret being so patronizing?

SATISFIED

Synonym: Contented, happy, gratified, appeased, pleased, fulfilled.

I'm sensing that you feel more satisfied with life lately -- what's going on?

SCANDALIZED

Synonym: Shameful, indecent, defamed, slandered, maligned, defiled.

You feel scandalized that she could have made up such a vicious story about you?

SCARED

Synonym: Frightened, afraid, fearful, intimidated, startled.

When they told you it had been a heart attack, you must have felt really scared!

SECRETIVE

Synonym: Private, personal, reticent.

I sense you are feeling secretive about what you know, but it sounds like a serious crime has been committed.

SECURE

Synonym: Safe, protected, assured, confident, guarded, firm, settled.

I'm hearing that the thing that makes you feel secure in this new relationship is her high personal integrity and self-respect.

SEDATE

Synonym: Quiet, composed, dignified, sober, calm, unruffled, formal.

So it is your music that makes you feel sedate; it is the most important thing in your life!

SELF-CONFIDENT

Synonym: Fearless, secure, independent, assured, positive, certain.

You are saying you felt self-confident when they asked you to give the presentation, but you have not been able to sleep since.

SELFISH

Synonym: Stingy, egotistical, tight, miserly, greedy, self-centered.

So you feel selfish taking care of your own needs, even though the majority of your time is given to others.

SELF-MADE

Synonym: Proud, confident, capable, self-reliant, independent.

Your reading, travels and experience make you feel self-made, but without formal credentials, no one will hire you?

SELF-RELIANT

Synonym: Independent, able, confident, autonomous, competent.

You are saying you like feeling self-reliant and you would rather die than go into the nursing home?

SERIOUS

Synonym: Solemn, earnest, sober, austere, intense, deliberate.

I can tell you felt serious when you wrote the proposal, but now after three rejections you are discouraged.

SEXY

Synonym: Desirable, attractive, sensual, lovable, passionate.

Are you saying you feel sexy most of the time, but your husband still insists on the lingerie?

SHAKY

Synonym: Unstable, uncertain.

You're feeling shaky about your trip to San Francisco; is it the rumors of earthquakes that's bothering you?

SHALLOW

Synonym: Superficial, frivolous, dull, foolish, stupid, trivial.

Deliberately choosing to flirt only with gorgeous men makes you feel shallow, but you can't seem to help yourself?

SHAMEFUL

Synonym: Corrupt, indecent, immoral, vulgar, unclean, sinful, dishonest.

It felt shameful to have to appear in the lineup; nothing like that ever happened to you before?

SHATTERED

Synonym: Broken, crushed, disloyal.

It sounds like you felt shattered when you found the 'good-bye' note - how can you pick up the pieces?

SHOCKED

Synonym: Startled, frightened, troubled, offended, dismayed, appalled.

So you felt shocked to learn that your husband is HIV+; you had no knowledge of his risky behavior?

SHREWD

Synonym: Astute, cunning, clever, tricky, ingenious.

When you closed the deal you felt shrewd, knowing all the time the problems they would be facing.

SHY

Synonym: Bashful, timid, humble, reserved, restrained, modest, coy.

It seems that you are aware that you are missing a lot of fun by feeling so shy - what would help overcome it?

SINCERE

Synonym: Honest, genuine, serious, reliable, trustworthy, earnest.

You felt sincere when you offered to baby-sit, but you forgot how much work pre-schoolers can be.

SINFUL

Synonym: Corrupt, unrighteous, evil, wicked, immoral, unjust.

You ate so much you actually felt sinful?

SKEPTICAL

Synonym: Doubtful, dubious, suspicious, uncertain, distrusting, cynical.

Your son-in-law promised again to stop drinking, but I hear that you are feeling skeptical.

SLEAZY

Synonym: Cheap, shabby, poor, tacky, pitiful, wretched, shoddy.

The dress he bought you makes you feel sleazy, but he is expecting you to wear it to the party tonight?

SLEEPY

Synonym: Tired, fatigued, drowsy, exhausted, weary, haggard.

Your only symptom is that you're feeling sleepy; how long since you took the pills?

SLOTHFUL

Synonym: Lazy, torpid, sluggish, apathetic, lethargic, indolent.

I'm sorry I said you felt slothful; I don't know what a sloth is either.

SLUGGISH

Synonym: Lazy, slow, lethargic,
            torpid, slothful, indolent.

Your ailing mother expects you to
do everything for her, and you are
feeling sluggish after six weeks
of caring for her.

SMITTEN

Synonym: Lovestruck, adoring, affectionate.

I sense that you're feeling smitten with this new man
in your life.

SMOTHERED

Synonym: Choked, breathless, extinguished.

His jealous questioning makes you feel smothered; you can't even have any friends anymore?

SOCIABLE

Synonym: Friendly, amiable, hospitable, warm, genial.

You say you feel sociable after three drinks, but she has another name for it?

SORROWFUL

Synonym: Grieved, afflicted, sad, dejected.

It makes you feel sorrowful to think those happy days are over.

SORRY

Synonym: Apologetic, regretful, penitent, repentant, remorseful.

You feel sorry that your friend's feelings are hurt, but you don't feel ready to make amends.

SPECIAL

Synonym: Distinctive, unusual, exclusive, unique.

When your kids run to greet you they make you feel special, and the hard day's work seems all worthwhile!

SPEECHLESS

Synonym: Dumb, mute, in awe.

The implications that you might somehow have been involved in the thefts left you feeling speechless?

SPENT

Synonym: Exhausted, weary, tired, consumed, finished.

You want to see the perpetrator come to justice, but the days in the courtroom have you feeling spent.

SPIRITED

Synonym: Lively, vivacious, effervescent.

I see that you were feeling spirited on the ice, and that you deserved those high marks from the judges.

SPIRITUAL

Synonym: Religious, holy, pure, godly, moral, divine, pious.

Spending hours alone in the chapel has you feeling spiritual, but you are wondering how to capture that in everyday life?

PITEFUL

ynonym: Vengeful, vindictive, resentful, hateful, angry, cruel, malicious.

ou have decided not to tell the rapist that you are HIV+ (positive)
ecause you feel spiteful, even though he might infect his wife?

PLENDID

ynonym: Wonderful, magnificent, beautiful, marvelous, glorious.

must have felt splendid to watch your daughter receive the gold
iedal on TV, but it has been a long time since you have seen her.

POOKY

ynonym: Weird, frightening, scary, alarming, mysterious, uncanny.

felt spooky entering the tunnels under the old asylum and recalling
ie inhuman treatment of years past.

QUEAMISH

ynonym: Queasy, uncomfortable, finicky.

ou say seeing the octopus on the buffet table made you feel
queamish?

TIMULATED

ynonym: Excited, encouraged, provoked, intrigued, energized,
            exhilarated.

ou were amazed at how stimulated you felt just holding his hand?

STODGY

Synonym: Boring, dull, wearisome, tedious, witless, vapid, insipid.

Trying to talk with the teenagers made you feel stodgy; it's like they speak a different language?

STONED

Synonym: Drunk, intoxicated, drugged.

All you remember is feeling stoned; everything else is vague?

STRAINED

Synonym: Pressured, stressed, cornered, forced.

It sounds like you are feeling strained by your work on the crisis line when your own issues are unresolved.

STRANDED

Synonym: Abandoned, deserted, forgotten, neglected, alone.

Allowing your son to use the car for the evening leaves you feeling stranded, even when you have no place to go?

STUBBORN

Synonym: Obstinate, unreasonable, tenacious, headstrong, persistent.

If you both feel that stubborn about the issues, what can we do to effect a resolution?

TUDIOUS

ynonym: Industrious, academic, learned, bookish, contemplative, thoughtful.

our dad wants you to go out for football, but you feel studious; what akes you happy?

TUMPED

ynonym: Confused, puzzled, bewildered, baffled, lost, speechless, befuddled.

Vhen we talk about where the drugs might have come from, it ounds like you feel stumped; are you protecting someone?

TUPENDOUS

ynonym: Grand, outstanding, marvelous, great, miraculous, breathtaking.

Vhen you received the gold medal, you felt stupendous, and ouldn't help wondering if your mother was watching?

TUPID

ynonym: Senseless, ignorant, dumb, irrational, absurd, mindless, moronic, inane.

ou felt really stupid when you made a joke about the tragedy and obody laughed.

UAVE

ynonym: Urbane, cultured, sophisticated, agreeable.

s you entered the dinner party, you felt suave; it must have been special moment for you!

SUBLIME

Synonym: Grand, noble, important, eminent, distinguished, prominent, lofty.

Seeing your work actually published must have felt sublime!

SUBVERSIVE

Synonym: Underhanded, rebellious, backstabbing, destructive, undermining.

Playing the office politics always makes you feel subversive; wha would happen if you refused?

SUFFOCATED

Synonym: Breathless, winded, smothered, stifled, strangled, choked.

Family life has you feeling suffocated; you miss the freedom of th open road?

SUICIDAL

Synonym: Self-destructive, deadly, harmful, lethal.

The diagnosis made you feel suicidal; all you see is six months c suffering and then death?

SUPERSTITIOUS

Synonym: Irrational, unreasonable, mystical, mysterious.

These rituals you perform make you feel superstitious, but you ar afraid to stop?

URPRISED

ynonym: Alarmed, shocked, amazed, astounded, dumbfounded, startled.

o you felt surprised when you ot the phone bill - you don't member calling Tokyo?

USPICIOUS

ynonym: Distrustful, jealous, unbelieving, doubtful, dubious, wondering.

sounds like you felt suspicious when he came home with his nderwear on backwards.

WINDLED

ynonym: Cheated, tricked, duped, deceived, defrauded.

n hearing that you felt swindled when your accountant was dicted for tax evasion.

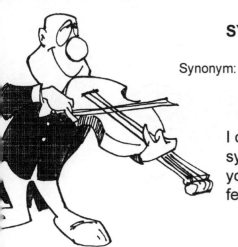

SYMPATHETIC

Synonym: Understanding, empathetic, sensitive, thoughtful, compassionate, pitying.

I can sense you feel sympathetic, but earlier you were saying she felt no remorse.

TAINTED

Synonym: Spoiled, contaminated, infected, diseased, polluted.

You have told me you feel tainted if someone even touches you, bu
you realize people touch each other all the time.

TEMPTED

Synonym: Enticed, seduced,
charmed, lured,
intrigued, influenced
persuaded.

When you found the wallet you
felt tempted to keep it, but were
moved by the pictures of his
family.

TENDER

ynonym: Warm, compassionate, thoughtful, kind, sensitive.

sounds like you feel so tender each time you speak of her; he must be very special.

TENSE

ynonym: Nervous, jumpy, distraught, anxious, excited, jittery.

can hear how tense you must have felt when you walked into the room and everybody stopped talking.

TENTATIVE

ynonym: Uncertain, unsure, wondering, indecisive, conditional, unsettled.

sense you are feeling tentative about his proposal; how do you think he would feel if you said that you needed more time?

TERRIBLE

ynonym: Awful, frightful, ghastly, horrifying, appalling.

When you realized how much you hurt his feelings, you must have felt terrible!

TERRIFIC

Synonym: Wonderful, outstanding, great, fantastic.

When your dad said you could build a darkroom you felt terrific, bu
it turned out to be just another broken promise.

TERRIFIED

Synonym: Frightened, shocked, horrified, stunned, panicky.

You looked up to see the
oncoming headlights and felt
terrified, then someone jerked
you out of the street?

TERRORIZED

Synonym: Intimidated, threatened, stalked, hunted, pursued.

Even after you told the police how terrorized you feel, they are sti
unwilling to go after the stalker?

THANKFUL

Synonym: Grateful, indebted, pleased, satisfied, beholden, appreciative.

You felt thankful that the doctor was able to stop the bleeding in time and want to repay him somehow?

THOUGHTLESS

Synonym: Foolish, unreasonable, senseless, inept, stupid, inconsiderate.

Pushing your way into the crowd for an interview made you feel thoughtless when you sensed the victim's pain.

THREATENED

Synonym: Endangered, imperiled, insecure, warned, intimidated.

There have been so many layoffs recently that you feel threatened -- are you worried that you may be next?

THRILLED

Synonym: Excited, moved, stimulated, touched.

You must have felt thrilled when Disney selected you for an interview - it's a chance of a lifetime!

TIRED

Synonym: Weary, fatigued, run-down, faint, wasted.

Just thinking about how much work it will take to clean up after the flood makes you feel tired.

TORMENTED

Synonym: Persecuted, abused, troubled, hurt, oppressed.

You felt tormented long enough; from this point on you say you don' care what happens to her?

TORTURED

Synonym: Abused, tormented, victimized, injured, mistreated, harassed.

As you sifted through the ashes of your burned out home, you fel tortured by the memories lost in the flames.

TOUCHED

Synonym: Moved, affected, stirred, impressed, sympathetic, influenced.

You felt touched by the story of her struggle, but now you are convinced she is just using you?

TRANQUIL

Synonym: Peaceful, composed, calm, unruffled, untroubled, gentle.

As you paddled slowly across the lake, you felt tranquil; but it still couldn't compare to what you were feeling for her?

TRANSFORMED

Synonym: Converted, changed, renewed.

You say you felt transformed after the beauty makeover, but your family ridiculed you?

TRAPPED

Synonym:　Cornered, helpless, imprisoned, confined, enslaved, restrained.

Despite his constant abuse, you feel trapped because you have nowhere to go; but there are places that will take you in!

TRICKED

Synonym:　Duped, cheated, bilked, swindled, beguiled, deceived.

He had a yard sale while you were at work, and you feel tricked that he sold all your stuff and disappeared?

TRIUMPHANT

Synonym:　Victorious, triumphal, successful, fortunate, exultant.

As you crossed the finish line, you felt triumphant, but that vanished when you saw the agony of those who lost.

TROUBLED

Synonym:　Bothered, harassed, annoyed, puzzled, perplexed, afflicted.

You felt troubled by the way he glares at you; you're afraid of what he might be thinking?

UGLY

Synonym: Unsightly, repulsive, homely, hideous, deformed, disfigured.

You felt ugly after the surgery, but then found the same love in his eyes that had always been there?

UNBALANCED

Synonym: Unsteady, deranged, unstable, insane, troubled, unsound.

You're ready to seek help; these changing moods make you feel unbalanced?

UNBEARABLE

Synonym: Intolerable, overwhelming, unendurable.

The thought of life in a wheelchair feels unbearable; you're not sure if you can go on.

UNBIASED

Synonym: Impartial, honest, fair, unprejudiced.

You say you feel unbiased in your hiring practices, but then the board pointed out your entire staff is white males.

UNBURDENED

Synonym: Relieved, lightened, set free.

Since she had been ill so long, you felt unburdened when she died; that doesn't mean you didn't love her.

UNCERTAIN

Synonym: Doubtful, dubious, unsettled, unsure, vague, undecided.

It sounds like you feel uncertain about taking the kids with you - what will happen if their father keeps them?

UNCOMFORTABLE

Synonym: Disturbed, annoyed, uneasy, restless, irritated.

You always feel uncomfortable in cemeteries, but were obligated to attend the funeral.

UNDESIRABLE

Synonym: Unattractive, unwanted, objectionable, distasteful, unlikable.

The mastectomy had you feeling undesirable until you saw the same tender love in his eyes that had always been there?

UNEASY

Synonym: Restless, uncomfortable, irritable, nervous, unsettled.

Something about his story has you feeling uneasy; do you think he's lying to you?

UNEMOTIONAL

Synonym: Numb, unfeeling, indifferent, apathetic.

You were feeling unemotional as you discussed your diagnosis, but went home and cried for hours?

UNETHICAL

Synonym: Immoral, dishonest, sneaky, unprincipled.

The new strategy makes you feel unethical; they have gone too far just to market a product.

UNFAITHFUL

Synonym: Untrustworthy, unreliable, deceitful, adulterous, unchaste.

Just your vivid fantasies of this other woman are enough to make you feel unfaithful?

UNFORGIVING

Synonym: Revengeful, unpardoning, ruthless, cruel, spiteful.

You finally feel unforgiving because he's gone too far and you're ready to prosecute?

UNFORTUNATE

Synonym: Unlucky, miserable, unhappy, afflicted.

So you feel unfortunate when you see what others have - have you tried counting the blessings you do have?

UNFRIENDLY

Synonym: Alienated, irritated, combative, vengeful.

Avoiding the neighborhood party made you feel unfriendly, but you didn't go anyway.

UNGRATEFUL

Synonym: Thankless, unappreciative, self-centered, unthankful, thoughtless.

You can't help feeling ungrateful knowing he's just going to throw it back in your face someday.

UNINSPIRED

Synonym: Unmoved, indifferent, apathetic, unconcerned.

It sounds like you feel uninspired by the negotiations; is a compromise possible?

UNINTERESTED

Synonym: Detached, indifferent, impassive, apathetic, unconcerned.

I'm hearing that you feel uninterested in a reconciliation, yet she pursues you?

UNLUCKY

Synonym: Unfortunate, ill-fated, afflicted.

You say you feel unlucky in love - could it be you've just been making poor choices?

UNMOTIVATED

Synonym: Lazy, apathetic, indifferent, indolent.

This ongoing depression has left you feeling unmotivated; how long has this been going on?

UNPOPULAR

Synonym: Disliked, unloved, scorned, avoided, despised, unaccepted.

Your child must have felt very unpopular when he wasn't invited to the birthday party.

UNPREPARED

Synonym: Surprised, inexperienced, unaware, unadvised.

It sounds like you feel unprepared for the family gathering at the funeral home, but know you are expected to be there.

UNPRETENTIOUS

Synonym: Humble, simple, unassuming.

You don't like the idea of the formal company dinner because you feel unpretentious and find them boorish.

UNPRODUCTIVE

Synonym: Ineffective, impotent, useless, sterile.

So you feel unproductive since being laid off; how can you fill your time?

UNPROFESSIONAL

Synonym: Unsuitable, inappropriate, improper, unethical, ignorant.

I hear that you felt unprofessional when you hugged the client, but that is just what she needed.

UNSETTLED

Synonym: Confused, uncertain, troubled, restless, unresolved.

You're saying you feel unsettled in the new town; how long have you been there?

UNSTABLE

Synonym: Unbalanced, changeable, unsteady, wavering, shifty.

You felt unstable when the officer asked you to walk a straight line, even though you'd only had one beer?

UNWANTED

Synonym: Rejected, outcast, unpopular.

It sounds like you felt unwanted when your mother repeatedly stated she should never have had you and your brother?

UNWILLING

Synonym: Reluctant, opposed, contrary, resistant.

I've checked with the shelter and they have room, but now you feel unwilling to leave?

UPSET

Synonym: Disturbed, troubled, worried, shocked, confused.

It sounds like you're feeling terribly upset - can you tell me what is going on?

USED

Synonym: Castoff, worn, old, abused, useless.

You must have felt used when they skipped, leaving you with all those bills?

VAGUE

Synonym: Unsure, cloudy, obscure, uncertain, perplexed, unsettled.

It sounds like you're feeling vague about the details; had you been drinking?

VALIANT

Synonym: Brave, fearless, courageous, assertive, steadfast, undaunted.

When you confronted the teens you felt valiant, but now you're worried they may retaliate?

VANQUISHED

Synonym: Defeated, destroyed, conquered, overcome.

That last creditor to call has you feeling vanquished; you can't go on working two jobs anymore?

VENGEFUL

Synonym: Vindictive, revengeful, spiteful.

When you found out he'd participated in the war protests, you started feeling vengeful - you still carry that pain after thirty years?

VEXED

Synonym: Troubled, worried, disturbed, annoyed, confused.

Her evasiveness about her past has you feeling vexed; what do you suspect?

VIBRANT

Synonym: Vigorous, energetic, alive, active.

You were feeling vibrant until your mother said you shouldn't have toys like that.

VICIOUS

Synonym: Wicked, cruel, evil, sinful.

Hurling the cat down the steps when you felt vicious now has you frightened?

VICTIMIZED

Synonym: Swindled, cheated, tricked, deceived.

This contractor took all your savings leaving you feeling victimized, and now you can't find him anywhere?

VIGILANT

Synonym: Careful, responsible, observant, watchful, alert.

When you called the police you were feeling vigilant, but now you're being prosecuted for harassment?

VINDICTIVE

Synonym: Revengeful, vengeful, spiteful.

When you threw away all her belongings, you felt vindictive; now you wish you had sold them?

VIOLENT

Synonym: Enraged, brutal, destructive, murderous, frantic.

Your neighbor's harassment has you feeling violent, but you know that can only lead to more trouble.

VIRTUOUS

Synonym: Honest, upright, worthy, moral, good, noble.

When you tried to explain the error of her ways you were feeling virtuous, but she became furious?

VOLATILE

Synonym: Changeable, unsteady, whimsical, fickle, frivolous.

Without the medication you feel volatile; one minute you're relaxed and the next you can't sit still?

WHIPPED

Synonym:　Tired, weary, exhausted, beaten, defeated.

You felt whipped after the group encounter, yet you say you learned a lot about yourself?

WONDERFUL

Synonym:　Ecstatic, excellent, amazing, incredible.

Admitted to medical school?　You must feel wonderful!

WORRIED

Synonym:　Troubled, anxious, concerned, distressed, disturbed.

I think I'm hearing you say you were feeling worried when your son didn't arrive on time.

WRETCHED

Synonym: Miserable, sad, distressed, woeful, afflicted.

It made you feel wretched when your own mother rejected you?

ZANY

Synonym: Wacky, humorous, funny, witty.

You love feeling zany but you do it so much, no one takes you seriously when you need a friend?

"Feelings" Products
from Community, Inc.
1-800-765-7417

TODAY I'M FEELING...

AFFECTIONATE

Call for Catalog!

CURIOUS
SPIRITED
ANGRY
HOSTILE
SORROWFUL
GRACEFUL
NAUSEOUS
BALANCED
SURPRISED

AGGRESSIVE
INDUSTRIOUS
BORED
EXCITED
FRIGHTENED
WORRIED
EXHAUSTED
COMPETENT
SLEEPY

"Feelings" Acrylic Desk Stand

Put up the feeling of the day with 35 laminated flash cards sure to express your mood.

Excellent gifts for staff, volunteers, family and friends.

HOW ARE YOU FEELING TODAY ?
Community, Inc.   1-800-765-7417

HAPPINESS

OPTIMISTIC   CURIOUS   LONELY   EXCITED   AFFECTIONATE   CONTENTED

AGGRESSIVE   SAD   EVIL   SPIRITED   SORROWFUL   CLUMSY

"Feelings" Coffee Mug

"*Feelings*" Products
from Community, Inc.
1-800-765-7417

Our Full Color, Laminated
"Adults" Feeling Poster!

"Feelings" Products
from Community, Inc.
1-800-765-7417

The "Kids" Version !
Also Full Color & Laminated

"Feelings" Products
from Community, Inc.
1-800-765-7417

IN FULL
COLOR !

FRONT

OUR 'FEELINGS'
T SHIRTS AND SWEAT SHIRTS
(Hane's Beefy T's)   (Lee's Heavyweights)

AND

BACK !

"Feelings" Products
from Community, Inc.
1-800-765-7417

FEATURING EITHER "KIDS" ILLUSTRATIONS (PREVIOUS PAGE) OR "ADULTS" ILLUSTRATIONS (THIS PAGE)

"Feelings" Products
from Community, Inc.
1-800-765-7417

Learning to Listen

JoAnn Yops
Illustrated by Michael Robinson

"Learning to Listen" is a comprehensive guide to the fundamentals of empathic listening and effective communication needed when we are called on to lend support and comfort to those who reach out to us. It also contains the basics of crisis intervention techniques and suicide prevention methodology. In addition, you will find our popular "Feelings" dictionary of 850 words and expressions included. 224 pp.

"Social Ecology" is an adventurous journey depicting what the human experience will be like when we begin to care enough about each other to allow everyone to simply participate. So many are left on the sidelines, bewildered by today's fast-paced, automated society. But with some simple changes, everyone can be accommodated and we all can profit immensely. This book is a world view for the future based on cooperation and a sense of community. 196 pp.

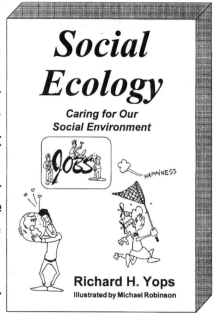

Social Ecology

Caring for Our
Social Environment

Richard H. Yops
Illustrated by Michael Robinson

Want to Make Money At Your Conference ?

It's a "Feelings" Store in a Box !

Or continually earn money for your agency or school organization ?

Community, Inc. offers sales of our products with big profits and no up front investment from you. Simply:

Step 1.   Call and order materials on consignment.

Step 2.   We ship materials so you can open for business.

Step 3.   You sell and take your profits off the top.

Step 4.   Pay us our regular store wholesale price plus shipping.

Step 5.   Return all unsold materials in good condition for full credit.

Earn up to 50 % with no up-front investment and no risk of getting stuck with unsold merchandise. Call today!

1-800-765-7417